WORK AND WELFARE

THE UNIVERSITY CENTER FOR
HUMAN VALUES SERIES

AMY GUTMANN, EDITOR

Multiculturalism and "The Politics of Recognition"
by Charles Taylor

A Matter of Interpretation: Federal Courts and the Law
by Antonin Scalia

Freedom of Association
edited by Amy Gutmann

Work and Welfare
by Robert M. Solow

Work and Welfare

✣ ROBERT M. SOLOW ✣

GERTRUDE HIMMELFARB

ANTHONY LEWIS

GLENN C. LOURY

JOHN E. ROEMER

EDITED BY

AMY GUTMANN

PRINCETON UNIVERSITY PRESS

PRINCETON, NEW JERSEY

Library of Congress Cataloging-in-Publication Data
Solow, Robert M.

Work and welfare / Robert M. Solow : edited by Amy Gutmann.
  p.   cm. — (The University Center for Human Values series)
  Includes bibliographical references and index.
  ISBN 0-691-05883-0 (alk. paper)
  1. Public welfare—United States. 2. Welfare recipients—
Employment—United States. 3. Poor—Employment—United States.
  4. Unskilled labor—United States.
  5. Wages—United States.
  I. Gutmann, Amy. II. Title. III. Series.
  HV95.S64 1998
  362.5'0973—dc21   98-6478

✣ CONTENTS ✣

❖ INTRODUCTION ❖

AMY GUTMANN

❖

LIKE THE right to vote, paid work has been seen by Americans since colonial times as "a primary source of public respect."[1] But unlike the right to vote, which was eventually extended to African-Americans and women, paid work is not generally viewed as an effective right of every able-bodied American citizen. Some people suggest that every able-bodied American who is willing to work hard and play by the rules can earn public respect and a wage adequate to support a family, but the best analyses of the American economy suggest something completely different. The American economy does not guarantee paid work for everyone who wants it, and the important work of raising children—of which there is more than enough to go around—is largely unpaid, and not a source of public respect in the way that a well-paying job is.

The major federal welfare program in the United States—Aid to Families with Dependent Children (AFDC)—was organized around cash payments to the poor who met various eligibility requirements. AFDC, which is generally associated with "welfare" in this coun-

[1] Judith N. Shklar, *American Citizenship: The Quest for Inclusion* (Cambridge: Harvard University Press, 1991), p. 1.

vii

try, never attempted to guarantee jobs to those who were willing and able to work. The aim of the American system of welfare has therefore not been to provide the conditions of public respect to all able-bodied citizens who are willing but unable to find work that pays (and pays enough to cover child care). Providing aid has been an alternative to providing work, and the values implicated by each alternative have been significantly different. Economists point to important trade-offs between work and welfare. This volume explores some of the most significant problems and prospects for American democracy of how this society evaluates the trade-off between providing work and providing welfare.

In the 1996–1997 Tanner Lectures in Human Values at Princeton University, sponsored by the University Center for Human Values, the Nobel prize-winning economist Robert Solow presents a strong yet subtle case for encouraging the movement from welfare to work by making work that pays available to every able-bodied citizen. Four other eminent thinkers—Gertrude Himmelfarb, Anthony Lewis, Glenn Loury, and John Roemer—offer commentaries on Solow's economic model of welfare reform. The model is guided by two explicit aims: one, to increase self-reliance among those citizens who are now on welfare, and two, to decrease the need for altruism among those citizens who now pay for welfare. Because self-reliance is such a positive value in American culture, the more citizens who see themselves and are seen by others as self-reliant the better. Because altruism is in such limited supply, the more it is conserved by public policies the better—provided it does not leave people out in the cold.

The conservation of altruism makes all the more sense in light of the apparently increasing reluctance on the part of American taxpayers to support citizens on welfare.

Although Solow's argument for welfare reform begins by aiming to increase self-reliance among poorer citizens and decrease the need for altruism among more affluent citizens, it ends by suggesting that a defensible welfare reform must take into account values other than increasing self-reliance and conserving altruism. Solow argues against increasing self-reliance, for example, at the expense of depriving children of their parents as caretakers, or depriving adults of a safety net to catch them if they fail to find (or to keep) an adequately paying job. Self-reliance pursued at all costs smacks of Social Darwinism, which Solow clearly rejects.

How would the value of self-reliance fare in the transition from welfare to a fair version of workfare? Citizens who now depend for their living on monthly checks from the government are obviously not self-reliant, but neither are most of us who do not receive welfare. We all depend on government and each other in many significant ways. In what sense would citizens who find jobs under a fair workfare system be more self-reliant? Some citizens who previously depended on the government for welfare checks would find work that pays a decent wage in the private sector, without any additional action on the part of the government, but other citizens would not. They would depend on the government for either creating new public-sector jobs or subsidizing the creation of new private-sector jobs. And some if not all citizens in both groups—those whose wages are too low to permit them to make ends meet—would depend on the tax system, perhaps in the form of an Earned Income Tax Credit, to increase their after-tax income.

The problem that Solow's version of fair workfare seeks to overcome is that welfare recipients appear to depend entirely on the government for their living, whereas everyone else appears to be at least to some extent self-supporting. The kind of welfare reform that is morally defensible—and the kind that Solow defends—aims for as many people as possible to make a decent living that does not depend entirely on government hand-outs or on private charity. Mutual dependency takes the place of complete dependency, and mutual dependency (unlike complete dependency) is the normal condition of citizens in a liberal democracy. *Fair* workfare, as Solow's discussion makes clear, is critically dependent upon society's collective willingness and ability to provide more jobs, better job training, and child-care facilities. Welfare reform of this sort raises the expectation that able-bodied people will work, but not that they will be completely self-reliant. Under a fair workfare system, most citizens are (and appear to be) mutually dependent.

Solow's case for welfare reform contains two important warnings. One is that fair workfare will "not come cheap," and those citizens who are able but unwilling to bear the costs should not pretend that they are being fair to those who cannot find a job. Only if welfare reform were as simple as getting people off of welfare and into existing jobs would altruism (in the form of willingness to have one's tax dollars spent on other people) be clearly conserved. But Solow agrees with Glenn Loury that welfare reform is far from this easy. For any morally defensible and practically realizable system to work, Americans need to demonstrate more willingness, not less, to help both themselves and others.

The second warning is that the move from welfare as we know it to a fair form of workfare will not transform people who are dependent on government into people who are self-reliant. What fair workfare can bring is far less conspicuous and complete dependency on government than now exists for many of the most vulnerable citizens. Inconspicuous and incomplete dependency is likely to be far less of a barrier to mutual respect among citizens; it is the condition not only of the poor but also of most citizens.

Solow summarizes a growing body of evidence that most welfare recipients themselves prefer work to welfare. This is true for both women and men, although women with young children recognize that workfare without subsidized child care and with no guarantee of decent wages would force them to sacrifice the welfare of their children. Even though fair workfare would cost more (at least in the short run) than welfare, it has two significant advantages relative to welfare: one, most welfare recipients prefer work to welfare (provided work covers the costs of child care and does not otherwise penalize them in relation to welfare); and two, public respect in this country has long been tied to having a regular job.

Fair workfare would offer citizens below the poverty line something that both they and most other American citizens value more than welfare payments, namely, a job that pays at least as much as welfare payments. Under fair workfare, citizens who need income support are obligated to work if—but only if—their fellow citizens fulfill their

obligation to enact public policies that provide adequate
employment and child support. The obligations under
fair workfare are mutual. Citizens who need income support are expected to work if they can, but only if their fellow citizens support programs that provide employment
and pay for child care. The mutuality of fair workfare reflects the ideal of reciprocity, which lies between self-
interest and altruism. Reciprocity expresses a sense of mutual responsibility among citizens, on the one hand for
contributing something to society by working, and on the
other hand for making sure that everyone who is willing
and able to work actually has an effective opportunity to
work. Reciprocity ties the responsibility to work on the
part of individual citizens to the responsibility on the part
of society to ensure the availability of both work that pays
a decent wage (either directly or through an Earned Income Tax Credit) and affordable child care for working
parents.[2]

Glenn Loury asks a critical question of advocates of fair
workfare: "But where does this leave the great number of
people who are not able (or willing) to 'work hard and
play by the rules'? Do they (and their children), then, deserve to be poor?" Answering these questions would be
easy for citizens who are relentlessly self-interested or
purely altruistic. Self-interest would say we need not
worry unless poor people threaten our welfare, and altruism would say we should put the welfare of others
above our own regardless of whether they are willing to

---

[2] Reciprocity and its practical implications for welfare reform are developed in more detail in Amy Gutmann and Dennis Thompson, *Democracy
and Disagreement* (Cambridge: Harvard University Press, 1996), chapters 2
and 8.

reciprocate. Reciprocity requires mutuality, when mutuality is possible. Children and people who are willing but unable to work deserve our support as we would deserve theirs were we similarly situated through no fault of our own. Those people who are able but unwilling to work—the so-called undeserving poor—are appropriately enough the parenthetical people in Loury's question. Even though the public debate often suggests that they are the norm, the evidence suggests that they are at most a small minority of welfare recipients. Until every able-bodied citizen has an effective opportunity to obtain work that yields a decent income (after child care), we cannot know how many individuals are really unwilling to work. The conditions that test willingness to work need to be instituted before the question of how to treat those who are unwilling to work becomes a practical one.

Anthony Lewis, following Alexis de Tocqueville, identifies the motivation of American citizens who support welfare not as altruism but as enlightened self-interest. Lewis suggests that enlightened self-interest recommends welfare over the alternative of living in a society in which mothers and children are begging on city streets for money from more affluent citizens. What is the "enlightened" part of the self-interest of someone who would rather be taxed more heavily than be surrounded by such poverty? At least some more affluent citizens sense that their interests reside not simply in themselves and their immediate families. Otherwise, as Lewis fears, all affluent Americans could choose to live relatively unperturbed in walled residential communities far away from such sights, or quickly and painlessly avert their eyes on city streets, or even look straight into the eyes of destitute people and not be terribly disturbed. The disturbing aspect of such sights depends on the sense that one's interests extend beyond oneself, one's family, one's friends, and even one's neighbors. For self-interest to be "enlightened," or reciprocal, people must care about how their fellow citizens are faring, and they must think it important (or at least act as if it were important) to contribute to their welfare as others contribute to theirs.

The problem posed by the trade-offs between welfare and workfare does not originate in adulthood. The roots of the problem extend back in time to the dramatically different life chances of American children, some of whom are born into circumstances that offer far lower odds of being able to hold a well-paying job than others. John Roemer develops an argument for greatly increasing the educational opportunities of the least advantaged children in order (among other things) to increase their productive capacity and therefore their earning capacity as adults. A leading non-neoclassical economist, Roemer provides a formal mathematical model based on neoclassical economics that supports Solow's informal analysis. In indicating the nature of the formal economic model and the quantitative assumptions that are implicit in Solow's argument, Roemer provides the beginnings of what could be a more technical extension of Solow's argument, one to which Solow himself subscribes. Other economists can now build upon this promising beginning. Roemer also further draws out the value implications of an effort to decrease the trade-off between work and welfare for those citizens who are least advantaged. Roemer suggests that the most efficient way of so doing is to increase the productive capacity of the least advantaged rather than give up on these citizens or offer them the second-best alternative of welfare.

The Victorian institution of the workhouse, Gertrude Himmelfarb reminds us, was designed to distinguish between the deserving and undeserving poor: the independent laborers on the one hand, and the able-bodied indigent on the other. The latter were deemed "less eligible" for public support and therefore consigned to the workhouse. The workhouse preserved the distinction between the two, Himmelfarb writes, so that the independent laborers "would not be tempted into a state of pauperism." If the workhouse also penalized people who were willing to work but could not find a job, through no fault of their own, then Victorian social policy is far more morally problematic than the focus on deterring people from becoming lazy paupers suggests. Himmelfarb aptly warns us that "there is no such thing as 'value-free' policies" and that "welfare is not a purely economic problem." With these admonitions in mind, two questions might be posed to critics of fair workfare. Were it not for the economic cost of instituting fair workfare, what justification would there be for denying welfare to a fellow citizen who in good faith looks for a job but cannot find one, seeks further job training but none is available, and seeks adequate child care but none is affordable? Is the added economic cost of fair workfare an adequate justification for a workfare policy that denies citizens in this situation a decent living? Solow's answer is unambiguously "no." His case for fair workfare combines ethics and economics.

✣ PREFACE TO THE LECTURES ✣

ROBERT M. SOLOW

✣

TANNER LECTURES are serious business. I was asked to choose a topic, and even outline briefly what I intended to say, about eighteen months in advance of the lectures themselves. "Welfare and Work" sounded just about right for lectures on "human values," especially because I had had, over the years, a particular sort of association with an important body of research on the underlying issues, from a slightly unusual angle. It seemed highly unlikely, at that moment, that a major welfare reform act—I cannot bear to write down the fatuous title that Congress gave it—embodying a fairly strong work requirement would already be law by the scheduled date of the lectures.

And now, six months later still, we are already hearing foolishly premature statements about the immediate effects and longer-run consequences of this particular version of workfare, both from the Congress that should not have passed it and from the president who should not have signed it. Keep in mind that some provisions have not yet come into effect; and anyway, the period since passage has been one of unexpectedly, even astonishingly, low unemployment, the sort of time when welfare rolls would normally shrink all by themselves.

The point of these remarks is that I hope these lectures

will not be understood as commenting on the 1996 legislation. I am aiming at a higher level of generality than that,
at the broad issue of mandating paid work as a precondi-
tion of or as a substitute for the receipt of welfare benefits.
I am interested only in some aspects of the contrast between workfare in one form or another and welfare as we
knew it. Other very important issues will be ignored entirely. A considered discussion of the welfare reform act
would require much more detail about its provisions.

Much of what I know about welfare and its reform
comes from my long membership in the Board of Direc-
tors of the Manpower Demonstration Research Corporation. MDRC has brought some serious science to the study
of interventions aimed at employing the disadvantaged,
where there used to be—and to some extent still is—a
desert of uninformed ideology. I am grateful to Judy
Gueron, the president, and to the whole staff, past and
present, of MDRC for years of superb adult education.
Professor Alan Krueger of the Princeton Economics Department sent me a number of sharp and useful comments, nearly all of which I was glad to incorporate. I must
also thank Professors Amy Gutmann, George Kateb, Paul
Starr, and Princeton University generally, for the honor of
an invitation to deliver Tanner Lectures, and for their
kindness, efficiency, and spirit during the time my wife
and I were at Princeton.

I have not dotted my text with bibliographical references, but there are a couple of debts to the literature that
simply have to be acknowledged. On social norms in general, I have profited from reading Edna Ullmann-
Margalit's *The Emergence of Norms* (Oxford: Oxford University Press, 1977) and Jon Elster's *The Cement of Society*

(Cambridge: Cambridge University Press, 1989). Neither book seems to me quite to provide what an economist needs, but they help. Much more to the point, I have read (an earlier version of) an excellent paper by Assar Lindbeck, Sten Nyberg, and Jörgen Weibull: "Social Norms, the Welfare State, and Voting," Seminar Paper no. 608, Institute for International Economic Studies (Stockholm, 1996). They pursue technical matters of budgetary equilibrium and majority voting that are not on my agenda, and they pay less attention to the uses of altruism. But their ideas and mine are exactly compatible.

WORK AND WELFARE

Guess Who Likes Workfare

ROBERT M. SOLOW

✥

I AM SURE that some of you are bemused by the almost oxymoronic character of the occasion. No doubt you recall Edmund Burke's gloomy thought that "the age of chivalry is gone, that of sophisters, economists and calculators has succeeded; and the glory of Europe is extinguished forever." You feel, wearily, that you know what he meant; it's that bad. A lecture—no, two lectures—on "human values" by an economist: one might as well invite a turkey buzzard to lecture on table manners. How would the poor beast know where to start?

I have to admit that many of my professional brothers and sisters do exhibit what Veblen would have called a trained incapacity to deal with human values in an unembarrassed way. But a concern for human values cannot do without economics. J. M. Keynes remarked that economists are not the guardians of civilization, but they are the guardians of the possibility of civilization. His Cambridge contemporary, Dennis Robertson, once gave a lecture entitled "What Do Economists Economize?" His answer was: love. He had in mind that altruism is scarce; there is never enough to go around. The function of economics is to devise social institutions that make it possible to economize on altruism and still live tolerably. Competitive markets, *when they function well,* are such an institution, with the remarkable capacity to transform individual actions motivated by simple greed into "efficient" and thus in some ways socially desirable outcomes. Then the limited supply of altruism can be saved up for those occasions when markets do not work well, or for those others when markets do their job but still leave us with outcomes that 51 percent of us—61 percent in the U.S. Senate—would like to improve, even at some personal cost to ourselves.

Robertson did not say, perhaps because he was not a middle-class American, that even if there is some left-over altruism available, its use may be unhealthy. In a society that places a high value on self-reliance, being the regular beneficiary of altruism may be dangerous to one's moral health. It can lead to unresisted dependency. That is no doubt one of the reasons why it is said to be better to give than to receive. (There is some moral danger in the other side of altruism too. Noblesse oblige is not always an attractive attitude in a seriously plebeian society.)

The general topic of these lectures—welfare and work—falls naturally into this category of questions. Unadulterated market outcomes leave some fraction of citizens, often including numbers of children, deeply impoverished; the question is what to do about that collectively, if indeed anything should be done. For some purposes it is important to know whether extreme poverty arises from a failure of the market mechanism or whether the system is working well but with unpromising raw materials. In one case the best long-run course might be to fix the market mechanism; in the other, the choice is between altruism and nothing. A lot of economics is about that large question, but I will enter on it only when it is directly relevant to the particular issues I want to discuss.

My aim in these two lectures is to locate the work-welfare alternative at the intersection of two social norms or virtues or "human values": self-reliance and altruism. My main point today is going to be that the total or partial replacement of unearned welfare benefits by earned wages is the right solution to the problem of accommodating those virtues in the kind of economy that we have. Welfare recipients will feel better because they are exhibiting self-reliance. Taxpayers will feel better not merely because less is demanded of their limited altruism but also because they can see that their altruism is not being exploited. The statement about taxpayers hardly needs arguing, so I shall take it for granted. But I shall spend a lot of time today making the statement about welfare recipients plausible by describing the words and the behavior of welfare recipients themselves.

Tomorrow I want to argue that carrying out the transformation of welfare into work will be much harder and more costly (in the budgetary sense) than anyone who sees its virtues has yet admitted. The standard discussion rests on the tacit belief that all the problems lie on the supply side of the labor market; kennel dogs need merely act like bird dogs, and birds will come. But that is a Panglossian error. The number of jobs is not a constant, but neither is it likely to respond one-for-one to the number of offers to work. To the extent that it responds at all, it will be as a result of forcing already low wages even lower; and that is precisely why the social norm of altruism leads

5

to the creation of welfare benefits in the first place. A contradiction or paradox seems to arise. There is a possible reconciliation, but it is not what current legislation envisions. So today my subject is welfare; tomorrow it will be work.

The United States has, like other rich countries, a complicated patchwork of devices for transferring tax revenues to poor people. The part of the system that is most often discussed pays cash benefits—welfare checks—mostly to single mothers and their children. There are other parts of the system—food stamps, Medicaid, housing allowances, and so on—but I will speak in a loose way only of welfare benefits, because I am interested only in one or two issues of principle, and not in the details. Everyone is aware that reform of the welfare system has been and may again be a hot, partisan, political issue. The recently passed legislation was bitterly fought over, and neither logic nor fact-based analysis featured strongly in the debate. No one can say with confidence what will happen in practice. The outcome matters intensely to the people involved. When you get very close to the limits of subsistence, little differences bulk large. Nevertheless, these lectures are not intended as a comment on current legislation. The small number of arguments I want to pursue should be equally significant whether you were born a little liberal or else a little conservative, or so I hope.

The particular form now taken by efforts to reform the welfare system is to eliminate as far as possible the passive receipt of transfer payments and replace it by a requirement to work, either as a condition for receiving benefits or as a total substitute for receiving benefits. There is also a movement to put limits to the length of time for which anyone can receive benefits, in contrast to the current rules that make eligibility—entitlement—simply a matter of meeting certain conditions. These proposals are actually more complicated in practice than they are made to sound in political rhetoric. In any case, they are not what I want to discuss; when I speak casually of "welfare reform" I will mean the intention to transform welfare into work.

If it could be taken for granted that welfare reform in that sense would be accomplished in ways that are neither punitive nor degrading, then it seems to me that the routine substitution of work for welfare would be clearly desirable, indeed a necessary step toward what Avishai Margalit has recently characterized as "a decent society." The reason is straightforward, and it has to do with human values. "In our culture" a large share of one's self-respect derives from one's ability to make a living. It is never an insult, not even a sly one, to describe someone as "a good provider" or "a hard worker" or even as a reliable "meal ticket."

One could go further and appeal to less casual sorts of evidence. It is a standard finding from survey research that much of an American's felt identity derives from his or her job. Occupational level is perhaps the most important single index of status, as perceived by oneself and by others. The occupational category "welfare recipient" is definitely not high on the list of designations that make a person feel good about herself. This is an important enough point that I will take time to document it directly.

I will start a little distance from home, and then come closer. The Canadian government is currently conducting an experiment it calls the Self-Sufficiency Project in two provinces, relatively prosperous British Columbia and relatively poor New Brunswick. The treatment being tested is not a compulsory substitution of work for welfare; it is an attempt to make work more viable for single parents. Those who choose to enroll in the program have one year in which to find a job or a couple of jobs that add up to thirty or more hours of employment per week. When they do, and for as long as they do for the next three years, they receive a supplementary payment that roughly doubles their earnings. The supplement is larger the lower the wage. It is on a very generous scale as these benefits go.

The short-run intention is to make market employment a more desirable option for welfare recipients with very low earning power, for some of whom unsupplemented work might mean an absolute reduction of income below what is provided by welfare. The long-run hope, of course, is that when the three-year time limit is up, many of the beneficiaries will have increased both their earning power and their attachment to work enough to keep them in the job market and off the welfare rolls. The Self-Sufficiency Project is a carefully planned, statistically sound, experiment. Eventually we will have a pretty good idea of its effectiveness and its cost. But that will not be for several years, and it is not what I want to report now.

What I do want to report is some conclusions from interviews with Canadian welfare recipients conducted by the research team that is following the project.[1] The un-

[1] Wendy Bancroft and Sheila Currie Vernon, *The Struggle for Self-Sufficiency: Participants in the Self-Sufficiency Project Talk about Work, Welfare, and Their Futures* (Vancouver: Social Research and Demonstration Corporation, December 1995). After the Tanner Lectures were delivered, I came across an

avoidable impression is that most of the women find their current position shameful, degrading, embarrassing. They are aware of being looked down on. They report trying to hide from other people in the bank the fact that the check they are cashing is a welfare check. The verbatim reports contain passages like this: "People call you 'welfare scum.' They look at you—all you ladies here in this room know—they look at you as if 'Hey, you're dirt,' right? And it's a very horrible feeling." Or this one: "You go out to any social event and people ask you what you do for a living . . . so you say under your breath . . . [mumble]. A lot of people think of you as being either lazy, or you don't care, or you're not educated enough." There is no doubt that most welfare recipients feel like losers.

On the subject of work, the researchers report as follows. "First and foremost, work was seen as the route to feeling better about oneself and having more control over events in one's life." The women say things like: "You get up in the morning and you know what you're going to do . . . you're confident." "You feel useful." "You don't have your hand out." "Even though it's peanuts . . . at least it's mine." "You get more respect from others." Then why do they remain on welfare? (It is called Income Assistance in Canada.) Some, of course, are disabled, some are going to school, and some have made a conscious decision to stay

---

interesting unpublished paper by Karl Moene (Economics, Oslo) and Michael Wallerstein (Political Science, Northwestern). Called "Self-Interested Support for Welfare Spending," it makes the point that a low-level means-tested welfare scheme will be unpopular if, as seems likely, the median voter is very unlikely ever to become a beneficiary. A universalistic scheme might generate stable support, and benefit a majority of voters. The authors point out that an element of altruism in voters' decisions could lead to different results.

home with preschool children. But they speak frequently of growing lazy, of having "a feeling of dependency that grows and grows." One of them said: "In the first few months of being on Income Assistance, you still have that incentive: 'I don't want to be doing this; I'd rather go out and get a job.' But when the job doesn't come, self-esteem gets lower. Then you realize, 'Oh, even if I do get a job, it's easier doing this.' And it does, it grows with time. You realize that you're pretty stuck."

There are no surprises here, unless you are one of those who think that all or most welfare recipients are happy-go-lucky exploiters of the system, or one of those others who think that the notion of dependency is the pure invention of unsympathetic right-wingers. The unshocking temporary conclusion I want to take from this recital is that a well-constructed substitution of work for welfare, provided it is applied humanely to those who are disabled or personally troubled, and provided it pays careful attention to the needs of children and the self-respect of adults, would be felt to be a step in the right direction by almost everyone, including those who would find their welfare benefits replaced by a requirement to work.

I chose to begin with the Canadian example partly to create a little distance, but more to elicit the reflex reaction: Ah yes, but those are Canadians (meaning "white people down on their luck"), and therefore not relevant to our problem. Indeed the Canadian sample has few if any blacks; the ethnic mixture contains about 10 percent "First Nations" and 5 percent Asian ancestry, more of both in British Columbia than in New Brunswick. Now comes the real point: there is exactly similar evidence from the United States. Beginning as long ago as 1983, states have been experimenting with work requirements for welfare recipients. In 1986, the Manpower Demonstration Research Corporation in New York interviewed a casual sample of participants in seven different states. Each of the states was operating a program of its own design, not all alike, but with a family resemblance to each other and to what would emerge from any current welfare reform. Unlike the Canadian experiment, these involved a mandatory work requirement, with sanctions for noncompliance. The states were New York, Arkansas, Virginia, California, Illinois, Maryland, and West Virginia, some high-benefit states, some skimpy. The interview sample was almost entirely female, predominantly Black and Hispanic (except for West Virginia and, to a lesser degree, Arkansas).

There is a lot to be said about the job-readiness of the participants, and other such characteristics. Here I want to report some attitudes, which seem to have been carefully elicited.[2] Across the seven states, 70 percent of those interviewed said that they were satisfied (either "strongly" or "somewhat" satisfied) about receiving benefits that are tied to a job, as compared with just receiving benefits. With some variation from state to state, again roughly 70 to 75 percent said that they felt better about getting welfare checks now that they were working for them.

More than 90 percent reported that they liked their jobs (most of which were subclerical or janitorial), and the same fraction looked forward to coming to work (to *those* jobs). Interestingly, fewer than a third thought that they had learned anything on this job. As a last touch, when

[2] Gregory Hoerz and Karla Hanson, *A Survey of Participants and Worksite Supervisors in the New York City Work Experience Program* (New York: MDRC, September 1986).

asked whether they thought that they or the employing agency was getting the better of the deal, three-quarters thought the employer was paying less than full value, 15 percent thought they were getting more than they were worth, and the remaining tenth thought it was a wash. So welfare recipients required to work feel more or less like the rest of us. The colonel's lady and Rosie O'Grady . . .

Another collection of cross-state interviews was collected in connection with the Job Opportunities and Basic Skills or JOBS program established under the Family Support Act of 1988. (The field of welfare reform is Acronym City; I am waiting for the first attempt to solve the unemployment and health-care problems simultaneously by a new System for Turning Unemployed People Into Doctors.) The difference is that this time single mothers were asked to make explicit comparisons of work and welfare and the choice between them.[3] The source of the general preference for working was confirmed. "I am determined to get off welfare. They treat you as less than human. Nothing is personal. I am tired of having to be accountable to welfare for everything that I do." Or: "To be self-supporting, independent, the personal satisfaction, working will be better."

When asked about the disadvantages of working for a living, the women focused on financial incentives and child care. "I was worse off when I was working than I am now. My rent went up and I didn't get any food stamps. My food stamps stopped in the first week of working and they were going to take my Medicaid away. Plus I had to

---

[3] LaDonna Pavetti, *Learning from the Voices of Mothers: Single Mothers' Perceptions of the Trade-offs between Welfare and Work* (New York: MDRC, January 1993).

pay for part of the costs of child care. My rent went up from $34 a month to $109. My highest check was for $110 a week, so one whole check would have to go for rent. On top of that I had to pay for gas, light and phone. When they told me I was going to lose my Medicaid, I quit working." Another said: "There's no job out there that would support us enough. And I wouldn't be able to spend time with my son. I'm glad for welfare because I can stay home and watch him do everything for the first time. I'd miss that if I had to work all day. And it's ridiculous that once you start working you don't get any benefits. I have a friend who works full time, six days a week, and never sees her kids. I'd love to get off welfare, but I'm not going to miss my son growing up just to get off it."

I want to include two more statements from these interviews, not for soap-operatic reasons but because they emphasize factors that must figure in any general model of the possibilities of welfare reform. One woman said, to explain her decision to enter a training program: "I walk everywhere trying to find a job and I can't find nothing. I've been all over. I can't find anything. I go down to the welfare office to look at their computer for jobs. I go all the time, but there aren't any jobs listed. I'm going to start a job training program. I'd like to work as a receptionist. They tell me after six weeks, they'll find a job for me. But we'll see." Indeed we will; the world is not full of jobs waiting for an uneducated ex-welfare mother to turn up. Finally I will quote from a woman who had worked for fifteen years after having been on welfare for ten years. The source doesn't say why she had to return to the welfare rolls, but the suggestion is that she had lost her job. "Going back on welfare was a nightmare for me. It didn't bother me when I first went on because I had no choice. It bothers me now because I had become independent. It's much harder to turn around and go back. Once you're totally independent of welfare you say 'I'm never going to do welfare again.'"

So far I have concentrated on revealed attitudes because I want to weave them into a more abstract description of the sort of equilibrium represented by a work-welfare system. Before I come to that, however, there is a factual question to be discussed. The voices I have been quoting come from women who are already involved in workfare, so they are not among those who are or might be excluded from work by disability of one kind or another. How do the welfare rolls divide between those who can work, by some reasonable standard, and those who cannot?

Here I take my evidence from a careful study of GAIN (Greater Avenues for INdependence—I warned you), which is California's version of a JOBS program. GAIN was enacted in 1985. It operates in all fifty-eight counties of the state, and is generally described as the largest, and one of the most ambitious, welfare-to-work initiatives going. The evaluation by MDRC studies six counties in detail, and will eventually include a five-year post-program follow-up comparing employment, earnings, and welfare receipt for those exposed to the program with the corresponding outcomes for those in a randomly chosen control group.

As part of this larger study, MDRC looked at GAIN participants in three counties who had spent two years or more on AFDC during the three years after entry into the program. This group already excludes single parents who were initially exempted from the program's participation requirement because of chronic illness, severe disability, or the presence of very young children. It is thus weighted in favor of those eligible to work.[4]

Indeed, more than half of them (57 percent) did work at unsubsidized jobs, and another 30 percent participated in job-search and training activities under GAIN, although they did not find jobs. Nevertheless, serious health and other problems were common in this group. The research team estimated that, on any given day, roughly one-fifth of this over-two-years group still on AFDC could not reasonably have been expected to work on that day, as a result of personal problems. If attention is restricted to the subset of the over-two-years group that never worked in the follow-up period, perhaps 27 to 38 percent of them could not reasonably have been expected to be at work on any given day. More than half of this group could have worked at some time, however. The research team concludes that although most welfare recipients—always excluding the clearly disabled and the mothers of very young children—could probably work at some time, many of them could not work steadily. Thus accommodating common, legitimate interruptions to work without harming families and children is a challenge to welfare reform.

It is worth separate mention that the group has at best low skills, so that most of them could qualify only for low-wage jobs, often unstable and without the standard fringe benefits. Other research starting at the employer's end of the market confirms that the jobs that tend to be available

---

[4] See James Riccio and Stephen Freedman, with Kristen S. Harknett, *Can They All Work? A Study of the Employment Potential of Welfare Recipients in a Welfare-to-Work Program* (New York: MDRC, September 1995).

in central cities generally require capacities and credentials not possessed by much of the welfare population.[5] The point to remember is that any considered attempt to substitute work for welfare will have to deal with a substantial minority of current welfare recipients who are capable only of sporadic work, and with a larger group whose earning power, even when fairly steadily employed, is very low by the standards of our society.

So far we have heard only from the receiving side of the welfare transaction. For symmetry one should explore the motives of solvent citizens (and their representatives) who vote to tax themselves to provide transfers to the working and nonworking poor. Luckily most of us are in that position, so we can conveniently ask ourselves. I do not pretend to any depth on this score; for my purposes, the impulse comes under the general heading of altruism, even if it includes an attenuated element of enlightened self-interest.

It goes without saying that these issues go back a long way. Charity, after all, is greater than faith and hope. It happens that just when I was drafting this lecture I was reading Professor Peter Brown's splendid *Power and Persuasion in Late Antiquity.* He describes how, in the fourth century, "the care of the poor became a dramatic component of the Christian representation of the bishop's authority in the community." The early Christian bishops assumed the role not only of "lover of the poor" but of protector and intercessor for the poor with the looming authority of the emperor. (In contrast, a friend who studies these things reports that ancient Jewish law, although

---

[5] Harry Holzer, *What Employers Want: Job Prospects for Less-Educated Workers* (New York: Russell Sage Foundation, 1996).

it insists on individual acts of charity, makes no provision for collective responsibility for the poor. Christianity marked a real change in this respect.)

I mention this not to pretend erudition, but as an occasion to show that some of the concerns of the modern welfare state were already present in the late Roman empire. Peter Brown tells of Firmus, a fifth-century bishop of Caesarea. One of Firmus's predecessors was the great Basil, whose many efforts on behalf of the poor included the building of a famous hospital and poorhouse. The poorhouse is mentioned in only one of Firmus's letters, in which "he declared his determination that it should not serve as a refuge for work-shy peasants fleeing from the estates of their owners." So welfare bums were a topic of conversation at the Club in Caesarea fifteen hundred years ago.

Closer to our time, the Victorians had a set of ideas about work and poverty, in some ways like our own and in some ways different. Perhaps Professor Himmelfarb will say something about that in her comments. I find that I do not have the gall to stand in front of her and summarize notions that I have picked up mainly from reading her works, especially since I would risk having got them wrong. My comments ought to come after hers, not before.

To conclude this lecture, and to set up the next one, I want to tell a slightly more theoretical story about welfare. The main building blocks are: first, an internalized social norm that values self-reliance, especially the earning of one's own living; second, a real, but limited, supply of altruism, itself the product of a social norm; and third, the existence, in any state of the economy, of a broad range of earning power, including a long lower tail of people whose earning power is at best inadequate to support a minimally respectable standard of life. (In putting it this way I must be assuming either that anyone who wants a job can have one, or that each person's potential for unemployment is somehow factored into the notion of earning power. Neither of these devices is better than an unsatisfactory dodge to postpone the issue. Job availability and unemployment will be the central topic of the next lecture.)

Now suppose that there is a prototypical welfare system that simply pays a specified—and presumably low— income to anyone who establishes eligibility by not having a job. In the presence of a social norm of self-reliance, people will sort themselves out between those who work and pay taxes, and those who do not work and receive benefits. The number of welfare recipients will depend on the size of the benefit, the frequency distribution of earning power, and the strength of the drive to earn one's own living. At this level of generality I will ignore such practically important matters as family circumstances, availability of child care, and the like. A natural-born economic theorist would include such things in a generalized "preference for leisure," and would avoid moralizing about it (not because morality is irrelevant, but because identifying a wish to stay home with small children as a form of laziness may not make for subtlety). The safer way is to ignore these questions, at least temporarily.

We know that most people, given the option of receiving the same $X a month, either as wages—net of the costs associated with working—or as handout, would prefer to work for their money. In this abstract model, the welfare rolls are made up of those whose earning power is considerably less than the standard benefit, enough less to outweigh the norm of self-reliance. There is a balancing between economic incentive and the work ethic. You may notice that I have been tacitly assuming the norm of self-reliance to be internalized in everyone to roughly the same extent. It is no doubt more likely that some people feel it more intensely than others. In that case a person is described by two characteristics: earning power and degree of self-reliance (not to be confused with *capacity* for self-reliance). A theoretical story can still be told, but it is more complicated because one needs to know the frequency distribution of pairs of characteristics. Since no one actually knows anything about that, the complication does not seem worthwhile. (If the characteristics are statistically independent, not much would depend on the complication anyway.)

It is important to keep in mind that an increase in the standard benefit would cause the welfare rolls to grow for two reasons. The first is just that more people would find the gap between their potential earnings and the welfare benefit too large to sacrifice. The second is more subtle: one has to suppose that the social norm favoring work over welfare is weaker, the larger the fraction of the population on welfare. Any social norm is strengthened by frequent observance and weakened by frequent violation. This dynamic may have more application to middle-class entitlements than to the welfare rolls, but that is another story. Within the model, any induced weakening of the norm of self-reliance will tip some marginal cases into the welfare pool.

Something has to be said about the motives of the majority who work and pay taxes and, most significantly, vote to maintain the welfare system, and to tax themselves to do so. They are, of course, the people whose earnings, after tax—and with account taken of the nonpecuniary satisfactions and troubles associated with their jobs, including, of course, the satisfactions of self-reliance—exceed the net benefits of welfare. I have chosen to say that they, or most of them, vote to support the welfare system out of "altruism," but that is obviously a catch-all for motives that may originate in religion, political philosophy, or inattention. In this context it simply means that most voters are prepared to sacrifice some private economic advantage so that those with the very lowest earning power should not have to live at the impoverished standard that their own wages could support. That motive is surely not constant; common observation suggests that it may be weakened by the observation that many people seem to violate the norm of self-reliance, or by the perception that the welfare benefit is relatively high compared with the earning power of many working citizens. It is easy to see how a politics of welfare can emerge and develop.

Now what would a work requirement do to this sort of equilibrium? Simply abolishing welfare reduces everyone at the bottom of the wage distribution to deeper poverty. It is a possible equilibrium if the working majority has grown resentful enough to lose whatever altruistic response it once had. The more interesting case is "workfare"—now welfare recipients are required to work for, say, the same benefit level as before. It is as if low wage rates are subsidized up to the benefit level, provided that the work itself is useful. The argument I have been developing suggests two sorts of consequence.

First, the welfare population will very likely be better off. It can achieve greater self-respect without loss of income. Remember the earlier evidence that people exposed to a mandatory work requirement quickly come to feel like regular workers, even a little resentful of the boss. (None of this holds unless the interests of children are given high priority. There is also a practically serious problem about the costs associated with working, including but not limited to the costs of child care. I will have a little more to say about this in the next lecture, but not much.)

Secondly, the work requirement may help to preserve the altruistic impulse of the majority by reducing both their tax burden and their general resentment at conspicuous violations of the norm of self-reliance. Alan Krueger has made the acute observation that the general popularity of the minimum-wage law and the Earned Income Tax Credit may reflect exactly the fact that they are both benefits that can only be got by working.

It is not clear a priori whether a work requirement would reduce the size of the welfare-workfare population. Bishop Firmus's work-shy might disappear from the books into criminal or other gray activity; but it is possible that others who had earlier chosen work over welfare, even at a cost in income, might shift to workfare just because the associated stigma might be less. What is pretty clear—again taking it for granted that the required work would have social value—is that the volume of "net uncompensated welfare payments" would be reduced by a work requirement.

One other important conclusion follows from this analysis. It has to do with the importance of what is called "packaging" for those who have adapted most function-ally to the world of work-and-welfare. If the end of "wel-fare as we know it" means simply the end of welfare, sim-ply throwing even the least capable onto the labor market to live off their earnings, the result is likely to be a higher incidence of abject poverty. The sort of idealized work re-quirement I have just been discussing is different: every capable person works, but welfare benefits (or a beefed-up Earned Income Tax Credit) top up the lowest earnings to allow a "decent" standard of living. Work is "pack-aged" with welfare.

This is what already happens anyway. Research has found that almost half of AFDC recipients, even without a requirement, now package work with welfare. Half of those piece together part-time wages and welfare benefits simultaneously; the other half cycle between work and welfare according to personal and family circumstance and the availability of jobs. Either approach should be seen as a way of living up to the norm of self-reliance.

The question of packaging will come up in the second of these lectures when I turn from the people who are sup-posed to find work to the work that they are supposed to find.

Guess Who Pays for Workfare

ROBERT M. SOLOW

✣

IT IS ONE THING to say, as I did in the first lecture, that the replacement of welfare by work would be a good thing for recipients, for taxpayers, and for the general reputation of public assistance to the poor. It is quite another question whether that transformation can actually be accomplished, and what it would then take to accomplish it. In particular, one is entitled to ask: what jobs will former welfare recipients find, and how will they find them?

This elementary distinction between desirability and feasibility is often neglected in political debate. During the rhetorical maneuvering that led to the welfare "reform" bill passed last summer, everyone seemed to be devoted to ending "welfare as we know it" but no one was prepared to describe how the new system would actually function. (Very likely "none of the above" would have been the most popular answer if the question had been asked.) Some time will pass before the shape of the new system is visible. The legislation left the main decisions to the individual states, who may well pass the buck to the large cities where most of the problem is, who may in turn pass the buck to the bishop of Caesarea.

That particular question is not on my agenda because I am not trying to understand the consequences of any particular legislative proposal. (That has already been done for last summer's bill by the Urban Institute, with scary results that do not seem to faze the bill's protagonists a bit, as well as by Peter Edelman in a recent *Atlantic Monthly*.)[1] My intention in this lecture is quite different from theirs. It is, first, to describe in theoretical but commonsense terms the consequences of withdrawing welfare benefits and forcing the former recipients into the labor market. What will become of them? Where will the jobs come from that they are supposed to find and occupy?

Then I will turn to the results of some experimental "workfare" initiatives on the part of several states, in order to get a quantitative grip on the employment and earnings prospects of former welfare beneficiaries and their successors. Finally, I will speculate briefly about what would be required for a successful transformation of welfare into work. My conclusion is going to be that we have been kidding ourselves. A reasonable end to welfare as we know it—something more than just benign or malign neglect—will be much more costly, in terms of budgetary resources and also in strain on institutions, than any of the protagonists of welfare reform have been willing to admit. And the reasons are normal economics.

On the question of job availability, there are two extreme positions to consider. The first is very optimistic: there is no problem. The jobs are there; they are always there. It is only necessary that those who seek them be

---

[1] Peter Edelman, "The Worst Thing Bill Clinton Has Done," *Atlantic Monthly* 279:3 (March 1997).

willing to accept realistic wages. Former welfare recipients, having nowhere else to go, will do just that. They will be paid what their productive capacity justifies, and that may be more than you think. The demand for labor is elastic; that means even a small reduction in going wage rates will generate a substantial expansion of job openings. And the implied clear presentation of a route to self-betterment will lead unqualified workers to acquire the education and training they need to move up the ladder. The small residue of genetic or accidental incompetents—the true paupers—can be left to private or public charity.

There is nothing illogical or incoherent about this story. It could apply to some worlds. I have to say that I do not think it describes our world, the sort of world that generated the 1982 recession in the United States and a decade of 10 percent unemployment rates, now even higher, in the main countries of Europe. It would be irresponsible, almost Alfred E. Newmanesque, to depend on this idealized story to smooth the transition to welfare as we will come to know it.

There is a another extreme theory that sees only rigidity where the first sees flexibility. It comes to deeply pessimistic conclusions. In this story, the total amount of employment is determined almost entirely by macroeconomic factors. Certain broad characteristics of the private economy, together with the stance of national monetary and budgetary policies, determine, within narrow limits, the aggregate expenditures of the final purchasers of goods and services. Most of the time the aggregate volume of production is limited by the amount of spending available to support it. The step from aggregate production to aggregate employment depends only on current productivity, a remote and slow-moving part of the macroeconomic equation.

It follows that the labor market is like a game, or several games, of musical chairs. (At my childhood birthday parties it had the more picturesque name of Going to Jerusalem.) When the music stops, the players scramble for the available chairs. Since there are fewer chairs than players, the losers are left standing. They are, you might say, unemployed. If the game were repeated, the losers might be different people, but the number of losers is determined entirely by the number of players and the number of chairs. Adding more players—which is what forcing welfare beneficiaries into the labor market would do—can only increase unemployment. Some former welfare recipients will find jobs, perhaps many will, because they are hungry, but only by displacing formerly employed members of the assiduously working poor.

I think that this story does not give enough credit to the adaptability of real market systems. Anyone who believed it would have a hard time explaining the fairly long periods during which the U.S. economy accommodates a growing labor force while the unemployment rate fluctuates within a fairly narrow range. The only possible explanations would be very good luck or very good policy, and you would have to be pretty gullible to find either one to be a plausible account of history.

Then how would a large-scale substitution of work for welfare play itself out in the real-world system of imperfect labor and product markets? A more accurate understanding will lie somewhere between the extremes I have just sketched. It will have to allow market forces to operate with some effectiveness, but will also respect the power of macroeconomic conditions over aggregate expenditure and output. This territory is still being fought over by mainstream economists, and I can not stop for subtleties. I will do the best I can.

Any effective transformation of welfare into work, if it means anything, must mean that a substantial number of unqualified people will be looking for work, who were previously not doing so. Some of them will find jobs just by being in the right place at the right time; they might have done so earlier if they had tried. These jobs will represent a net addition to aggregate employment. One sometimes gets the feeling that this is what some members of Congress visualize, and all that they visualize. If so, they cannot be right. There is absolutely no reason to believe that our economy holds a substantial number of unfilled vacancies for unqualified workers. The machinery of adjustment must be something more elaborate. Here and later, it is worth keeping in mind a point recently emphasized by Christopher Jencks.[2] There are substantial cash costs associated with going to work, largest for the mothers of small children. For that reason, many welfare recipients who do find work will find themselves worse off, perhaps substantially so.

The most immediate route by which the ex-welfare population can find jobs is by competing with and displacing other unqualified workers who are already employed, either by being in some way a more suitable employee or, more likely, by offering to work for less than the incumbent is getting. Unqualified workers are presum-

[2] "The Hidden Paradox of Welfare Reform," *American Prospect* no. 32 (May–June 1997), pp. 33–40.

ably excellent substitutes for one another, so only a very small wage cut would be needed. But pure displacement is just musical chairs: more players and the same number of chairs.

More important is the possibility that competition for jobs by ex-welfare recipients and their successors will drive down the wage for unqualified workers by enough to induce some employers to hire them to replace slightly more qualified incumbents who do the job better but have to be paid more. Since bottom-end workers are less than perfect substitutes for second-level workers, the fall in the unskilled wage will have to be perceptible to make the switch profitable for employers. There is displacement going on here too, but it is somewhat better than one-for-one because unqualified workers are, by definition, less productive than second-level workers. Also, a broader wage reduction for lowest-level *and* second-level workers has a better chance of expanding the number of employment opportunities available in that segment of the labor market. So there would be a small gain in total employment, but it comes at the expense of the earnings and job prospects of previously employed second-level workers. (This talk of discrete levels of skill is just an artificial simplification of a more complex process of job search by individuals and occasional matches with firms. It helps keep the discussion orderly.)

In principle, the process does not stop there. The erosion of the wages of second-level, slightly skilled, workers makes them more competitive with third-level, slightly more skilled workers. The fact that some second-level workers have been displaced into unemployment may lead to a further bidding-down of third-level wages as the competition for jobs intensifies. So the costs of adjusting to the influx of former welfare recipients spreads to the working poor, the working just-less-poor, and so on, in the form of lower wages and heightened job insecurity.

There is, of course, a long, branching hierarchy of skill levels in a modern economy. Each level is subject to competition from those just above and below, especially below. But one would naturally expect the degree of displacement to attenuate as one gets further and further away from the relatively unqualified former welfare recipients whose appearance on the job market is the source of the disturbance. By the time you get to the very top of the food chain, say the Princeton Philosophy Department, no one will be feeling any pain, and in fact the tenured members may be able to get their yard work done more cheaply. The adjustment costs will be concentrated at the bottom of the job hierarchy and the bottom of the income distribution. Of course it could be said that those are the very people who have been protected from competition all along by the unreformed welfare system. It is not a remark I would choose to make myself, but there must be some truth to it.

All this reshuffling in the labor market must have macroeconomic implications. The relevant question is whether any of them hold the promise of an easier transition to a world in which work has replaced welfare. Suppose we imagine the displacement and wage-reduction process to have worked itself out completely. The result is a lower economy-wide real wage. Can we expect that interim fact to generate enough net new jobs to accommodate the addition to the labor force created by the end of welfare as we know it? Or will there just be more unemployment?

It may help to think about two rather different varieties of unemployment. These correspond roughly to the two extreme theories I sketched to introduce this discussion. One sort of unemployment arises because there is not enough demand for the products of labor. Spending on goods and services is somehow inadequate. This is often called "Keynesian" unemployment. The other sort arises because, through one mechanism or another, wages are too high. Business firms could produce and sell more, but it would be unprofitable for them to do so. The way to expand production and employment is to have lower costs; for the economy as a whole, that means mainly lower labor costs. This is often called "classical" unemployment.

Classical unemployment will respond to wage reduction, though the process may be more complicated than this simple statement indicates. Keynesian unemployment may not respond; there is even a danger that a transfer from wage earnings to profits might result in lower total spending, which would be perverse for jobs. (This, too, is more complicated than it sounds.)

To come back to our particular problem, the issue is whether lower wages, on average, will more or less automatically provide new jobs to be filled by former welfare recipients and their successors. That turns on the responsiveness of the aggregate demand for labor to the real wage. There has been quite a lot of research on that very question, because the answer is of great general importance. I think it is fair to say that the measured responsiveness has been disappointingly small. (I say "disappointingly" because life would be easier if small real-wage changes could induce substantial shifts in employment, and if the same were true of other prices and the associated quantities.) It is not easy to characterize the range of estimates numerically, but it would not be far off to say that as much as a 2 or 3 percent change in the real wage level would be needed to elicit a 1 percent change in the demand for labor (in the opposite direction, of course). This result could be taken to reflect the relatively small weight of classical unemployment in the total, in the United States at least, or it might be telling us something about the working of labor-market institutions. In any case, the implication is that it would take a reduction of 3 to 5 percent in the average real wage to generate net new jobs equal to two-thirds of the adult AFDC population.

Is this a lot or a little? The first thing to say is that the required change in the national average wage is not the figure that matters. I hope I have made it clear that the competition for jobs set off by welfare reform would be concentrated at the lower end of the job hierarchy. It is certain that a perceptibly larger reduction in the wages of unskilled and semi-skilled workers would have to take place if the bottom end of the labor market had to absorb an additional million and three-quarters relatively unqualified workers. I would not want to say more than that, not at the university with the best collection of labor economists in the country. But it seems likely that unskilled wages would have to fall by considerably more than 5 percent. If conventions of equity or propriety, or the existence of a statutory minimum wage, should prevent the required reduction in unskilled wages, the consequence would be higher unemployment. Either way, the working poor will pay.

The more important observation is not numerical at all. Apart from magnitudes, the argument leads to the conclusion that the burden of adjusting to any genuine replacement of welfare by work will fall primarily on low-wage workers, especially those virtuous ones who have been employed all along. The burden will take the form of lower earnings and higher unemployment, in proportions that are impossible to guess in advance. It would be too drastic to imagine that the process might lead to the growth of a distressed class of very-low-wage workers and, through the workings of altruism, to the re-creation of welfare as we knew it. There are alternatives, to be discussed briefly later on. But I hope it is not drastic at all to doubt that many reasonable people who favor welfare reform have had in mind the imposition of nontrivial additional impoverishment on the industrious working poor.

Completeness requires me to mention one other way in which macroeconomic forces might ease this problem. Just because the addition of a million and a half or so new workers to the labor force represents some potential unemployment, perhaps the Federal Reserve might see it as some additional protection against inflation. Any consequent easing of monetary policy—or other macroeconomic policy, if there were any—could lead to lower interest rates, economic expansion, and better job prospects. I think this is a forlorn hope, however. Wage-induced inflation does not come from excessive tightness in the market for unskilled labor, but from better-skilled, higher-wage, sometimes unionized workers, if it comes from the labor market at all. The economy will not be measurably more inflation proof, and will have to work it all out on its own.

I say this despite the tendency for wage compression to occur in business-cycle upswings, that is, for low-end wages to rise proportionally more than high-end wages in good times. My guess is that this may happen because higher-end wages are more likely to be governed by long-term agreements, explicit or implicit, whereas low-end wages are free to respond to immediate market forces. It seems wholly unlikely that unskilled wage-push plays much of an independent inflationary role. Then an influx of former welfare recipients will not give the Federal Reserve much of a cushion against overheating.

Beyond these rather general considerations, there is some more direct evidence about the probable fate of welfare recipients forced into the labor market by the withdrawal of support. Most of it comes from the "workfare" experiments designed and operated by many states during the past decade. The most useful for my purpose are those that were conducted as genuine experiments, with participants assigned at random to the program itself or to a control group. The intake into the process consisted entirely of participants in or applicants to AFDC: experimentals were subject to the particular workfare program being tried out, while controls continued in AFDC, subject to the normal regulations. Differences in outcomes can thus be imputed to the effects of whatever mandatory requirements were imposed by the workfare program being tested. It cannot be assumed that these experiments anticipate the likely outcome of an all-out imposition of time limits, work requirements, or simply the closing-down of

AFDC. They do give us some quantitative insight into the likely fate of welfare recipients tossed into the open labor market.

I shall use as my main example the California GAIN (Greater Avenues for INdependence) experiment to which I referred in the first lecture. It is the largest and best documented of the state initiatives; and MDRC has collected and analyzed data extending out to three years after experimentals' first exposure to the program.[3] Longer-term observations are still to come. The program itself is complex; I will give only a brief and crude description and then cut to the chase. Upon assignment to the program, a welfare recipient or applicant who lacks a high-school diploma or a GED certificate (General Educational Development, probably worth very little), or scores low on a basic skills test, or is deficient in English, is assigned to one or another basic education scheme. Others, and those who finish their basic education, move on to an organized job-search activity. This includes training sessions in which groups are taught basic job-seeking and interviewing skills, and then supervised job search, with telephone banks, job listings, and some counseling. This goes on for about three weeks. Those who do not find a job in this way proceed to form an individual employment plan, working with a counselor. The plan will entail further activities, like vocational training, unpaid work experience, and so on. These activities then alternate with job search.

The question is: what is the subsequent labor-market

[3] The results are reported in James Riccio, Daniel Friedlander, and Stephen Freedman, *GAIN: Benefits, Costs, and Three-Year Impacts of a Welfare-to-Work Program* (New York: MDRC, September 1994).

history of those subject to these requirements, particularly but not only as compared with the controls who simply carry on as before? We can answer this question for six miscellaneous California counties. One of them, Riverside, between Los Angeles and San Diego, is especially interesting because it is an outlier, in which the program was conducted by its staff in a very energetic and aggressive way. Here are the key results, taking all six counties together, a total of 17,677 experimentals and 5,114 controls. During each of the three years of follow-up, about 40 percent of the experimentals had some employment. These were not steady jobs; in the last quarter of the third year, only 28.5 percent had any employment, and of course the proportion employed in any month or week would be still smaller. All told, 56.7 percent of the experimentals held a job at one time or another during the three-year period. Almost 51 percent of the controls had some employment during that time, so the net impact of the GAIN program was to increase the fraction ever employed by 6 percentage points. This difference is statistically significant, but it is fairly small.

The conclusion to be drawn is this: in California, in the economic conditions of the early 1990s, about a third of welfare recipients held a job at one time or another during any year; participation in the GAIN version of workfare increased that fraction by 4 to 6 percentage points. One cannot be sure that this small margin is an indicator for the future, but the burden of proof is on anyone who thinks that welfare recipients forced into the labor market will be very successful in the search for jobs.

I mentioned that Riverside County seemed consistently to get better results than any of the other five counties. It is worth seeing how much better, as an indicator of the best that might be hoped for. In one sense the comparison is a source of optimism. Riverside did do better than the other five counties; so it does matter how a welfare reform program is conducted, and activism pays off. That is the good news. The bad news is that even the Riverside results suggest that the job prospects for former welfare recipients are pretty grim.

Two-thirds of the Riverside experimentals held a job sometime in the first three years of their exposure to GAIN, 10 percentage points more than the average for all six counties. And the difference seems to have nothing to do with the Riverside area itself, because the control group in Riverside had the same experience as the statewide average. So the conduct of the program is the key. But the Riverside advantage diminished year by year and, besides, although it is big enough to be noticed it is not big enough to solve the problem.

I could report on similar studies of the work-welfare experiments conducted by a dozen other states. But the basic message would be unchanged. The various states have tried slightly different programs, in slightly different economic environments, and naturally they produce slightly different results. But none of them offers grounds for optimism about the ability of welfare recipients to find and hold jobs, or to earn a decent living. (Some are more pessimistic in their implications than the California GAIN experiment.)

Instead I shall describe briefly a much smaller and more casually studied episode in Michigan, because it replicates more nearly the effects of a pure-and-simple end to welfare benefits.[4] Until its termination in October 1991, the state of Michigan had funded a program called General Assistance that paid cash benefits of $160 a month to nonelderly poor adults without dependent children. The authors of the study note that this population was probably more rather than less able to find and keep jobs than the standard AFDC population. General Assistance was ended in October 1991. (Most of the recipients had been receiving, and continued to receive, other benefits.)

A representative sample of 426 ex-recipients of General Assistance were interviewed two years after the program had ended, and were asked about their labor-market experience in the meanwhile. About 65 percent of them had worked at a regular job or at casual labor at some time during the period. This frequency was the same for those with less than a high-school degree and those with a high-school diploma, a GED certificate, or more. The better-educated group held significantly steadier and better-paid jobs, however. For instance, 46 percent of them were employed in the month of the survey, compared with 28 percent of the high-school dropouts, at average hourly wages of $6.07 and $4.78, respectively. Their total earnings in the month before the survey averaged $596 for the better-educated and $377 for the less-educated, which implies that the two groups averaged about 100 and 80 hours of work, respectively in that month. (Full-time work would be about 160 hours.)

[4] The analysis is reported in Sandra K. Danziger and Sheldon Danziger, "Will Welfare Recipients Find Work When Welfare Ends?" in *Welfare Reform: An Analysis of the Issues,* edited by Isabel V. Sawhill (Washington, D.C.: Urban Institute, 1995), pp. 41–44.

Those who worked in the survey month, even the high-school dropouts, earned more than the old General Assistance benefit of $160. But it could not be said that they earned a living. It would be a gross overestimate even to multiply $377 per month by twelve to get $4500 because a third of the sample never worked at all during the two years, and very few of those who worked were able to work steadily. The high-school educated did better, but for the same reasons, $7200 a year would considerably overestimate the earning capacity even of those who succeeded in finding work at all.

The indications from Michigan and California are in the same ballpark. Without some added ingredients, the transformation of welfare into work is likely to be the transformation of welfare into unemployment and casual earnings so low as once to have been thought unacceptable for fellow citizens.

More microscopic, almost ethnographic, observations only add depth to this picture. William Julius Wilson has powerfully documented the disappearance of jobs from poor, black inner-city neighborhoods like the South Side of Chicago.[5] Katherine Newman, herself an anthropologist, followed up all job openings filled by four fast-food franchises in Harlem in 1993, and interviewed those who got the jobs and those who applied but failed. (There were fourteen applicants for each job filled.) The winners in this sweepstakes were better educated and better connected than the losers, but even the losers were more experienced and more educated on average than the typical welfare recipient. Three-quarters of the losers were unemployed

[5] William J. Wilson, *When Work Disappears: The World of the New Urban Poor* (New York: Knopf, 1996).

when interviewed a year later, although most of them had continued to look for work.[6] It is impossible to believe that the forced influx of ex-welfare beneficiaries into these labor markets could do anything but make a bad situation worse. (By the way, preliminary results from the Canadian Self-Sufficiency Project confirm this pessimism.)

The proper conclusion from this analysis is not that the substitution of work for welfare, however desirable it may be, is infeasible in practice. That might be so if the only alternative to welfare as we know it were simply to walk away from it. More to the point, I think, is the conclusion that a decent welfare-to-work transition will require a more complicated—and more expensive—set of changes. Two policy conclusions, in particular, seem to me to follow from the argument of these lectures.

The first is that an adequate number of jobs for displaced welfare recipients will have to be deliberately created, either through some version of public-service employment or through the extension of substantial special incentives to the private sector (profit and nonprofit). Appeals to businesses to hire welfare recipients voluntarily are a form of abdication of responsibility, and even subsidies to employers are likely to run into real problems of management. There will have to be a determined and expensive effort to increase the demand for unskilled and unqualified labor.

William Julius Wilson has advocated the re-creation of something like the WPA of the New Deal years. I can see

[6] See Katherine Newman and Chauncy Lennon, "Finding Work in the Inner City: How Hard Is It Now? How Hard Will It Be for AFDC Recipients?" Working Paper 76 (New York: Russell Sage Foundation, October 1995).

the point of that. Pretty clearly there are major infrastructure needs in urban and rural communities that could be met with little or no trespassing on the private sector, and with intensive use of unskilled labor. But there are two ways in which this suggestion seems to fall short of the need. Wilson is thinking mainly about males trapped in inner-city ghettos without employment opportunities. But the AFDC population is primarily female, often women with children. Unskilled construction labor may be a mismatch if the goal is to insert that group into the world of work and to build up marketable skills.

The second deficiency is related. In an economy that has been durably trending toward the production of services instead of tangible goods, focusing on heavy construction is like trying to make water flow uphill. It would seem more useful to create an employment track that led to work habits and skills normally in demand in the service sector. This would also be a better match with the gender composition of the welfare population. There are no big-time models for such an effort, but some institutional ingenuity might find a way.

The main point, however, is not the design of a particular scheme. It is, as Wilson sees, the need for purposeful creation of jobs, in numbers, places, and forms that are suitable for the people who will fill them, and that can provide the sort of experience that may eventually have cash value in the open labor market. Any scheme that will do the trick will be costly, in budgetary dollars and in the need to invent and to staff institutions of a kind for which we have little experience or even intuition. The task is even harder than it sounds, because it involves swimming upstream. There has been in recent years a massive shift in demand away from unskilled labor. The source appears to have been mostly technological, but the source is less important than the fact, and the fact suggests that the labor market will not naturally welcome an influx of unskilled workers.

The second conclusion I want to draw goes back to the notion of "packaging" that I planted toward the end of the first lecture.[7] Suppose we succeed in managing a transition from welfare to work. The evidence implies inescapably that the jobs obtainable by former welfare recipients will pay very low wages and pay them irregularly. (The irregularity inheres partly in the job and partly in the situation of the jobholder, as we have seen.) I think it is legitimate for taxpayers to want welfare recipients to work, but not so legitimate to want them to live at the miserable standard their earning capacity can provide, least of all if children are involved. The implication is that packaging will have to continue, and should be planned for. This means, by the way, that time limits are incompatible with the substitution of work for welfare.

It was observed in the first lecture that a large fraction of welfare beneficiaries today either alternates between work and welfare or does both at the same time. That pattern will have to be recognized as normal, even as a good thing under the circumstances. It should be regularized and institutionalized, to see that the incentives point in the right direction and that justice is done, and to guard against corruption. (Corruption is also a danger in any

---

[7]On this, see Roberta Spalter-Roth, Beverly Burr, Heidi Hartmann, and Lois Shaw, *Welfare That Works: The Working Lives of AFDC Recipients,* Report to the Ford Foundation (Washington, D.C.: Institute for Women's Policy Research, February 1995).

scheme of public employment. I have not dwelt on that fact only because corruption is a danger in any human social activity, perhaps even the Tanner Lectures on Human Values.)

The institutional details can be important. Here we have the advantage of an already functioning mechanism, the Earned Income Tax Credit. It could be calibrated to provide a tolerable standard of living for ex-welfare recipients—and others—who work hard and play by the rules, to use another of those phrases. Employers should understand that they benefit from the EITC too, because, like any subsidy, it puts a little downward pressure on the market wage.

The object of this mixed system should be to achieve a reasonable equilibrium between the norms of self-reliance and altruism. The real trouble with welfare as we knew it is that it tended to erode both. My suggestion is that a mixed work-welfare system, with an adequate supply of jobs, stands a chance of reinforcing both self-reliance and altruism, but such a system will not come cheap. There has been no sign yet that the United States is willing to put the necessary money where its mouth is.

Suppose nothing special happens. Welfare "reform" follows the script, without any amelioration. What will we then think about it? The welfare rolls will diminish. Governors will point with pride. Congressmen and senators (and presidents?) will nod their satisfaction. No one will ask what has happened to the former welfare recipients or to the working poor. If anyone asks, there will be no answer. There will be no data. As Alan Krueger pointed out to me, the relevant experiments will not have been performed; the administrative system tracks only recipients, not the would-have-beens. They may be living with relatives who cannot afford them, or on the street, or under the bridges of Paris. The need for relevant data is not just the peculiar craving of academic social scientists. It is the life-blood of rational social policy and its evaluation.

GLENN C. LOURY

❖

For my purposes it will be helpful to summarize Professor Solow's argument as follows: in thinking about public policies dealing with the poor, a conflict exists between two important human values—self-reliance and altruism. In the context of welfare, establishing a quid pro quo rooted in work can help to resolve the conflict between these values. Both those who give (taxpayers) and those who receive (welfare dependents) feel better about the transaction if recipients work for their benefit. Yet, there are problems with this resolution. Among the recipients there are young children to be cared for, the level of work experience and employment skills are low, potential earnings even from full-time year-round employment are meager, and there are physical and psychological disabilities that impede the finding and holding of a job. Inevitably, not all of the recipients will find jobs, and even fewer will keep the ones they find. Therefore, although the conflict of values can, in principle, be resolved through work, this will happen in practice only if assistance is given to recipients, including the creation of public-sector jobs, the provision of wage supplements, and the provision of services like child-care and health-care benefits, counseling, and training. In short, only if work for welfare recipients is properly supported can the quid pro quo of workfare provide a decent resolution of the tension between the competing values of self-reliance and altruism.

My principal response to this argument takes the form of a question: is "work" the appropriate lens through which to approach the conflict of values associated with the existence of dependent persons in our midst?

AT THE RISK of oversimplification, let me divide the issue of "work" for low-skilled persons into two subthemes— there are not enough low-skilled jobs, and people can't live on the wages paid in the jobs that are available. Of course, since demand curves slope downward, these issues are not independent. (That is, inevitably there will be a trade-off between the number of jobs and their remuneration.) But we can distinguish these two issues for the purposes of this discussion.

As Professor Solow recognizes, the shortage of suitable jobs for welfare recipients reflects both the slackness of low-wage labor markets and the characteristics and behavior of welfare recipients. He cites the work of anthropologist Catherine Newman of the Kennedy School at Harvard, which illustrates how, among relatively low-paid workers with skills clearly superior to the average welfare recipient, jobs are hard to come by, and hard to hold on to. (Thus, three-quarters of a Harlem sample of high-school graduates were unemployed one year after the initial interview, though the entire sample was selected from people actively seeking work.) He also cites the very modest positive effects of experimental efforts to find jobs for welfare recipients in California as evidence that many in this (welfare-receiving) population will have great difficulty holding onto jobs even if they can find them. As for the second problem (low wages), Professor Solow avoids advocating raising the minimum wage, but instead urges wage subsidies through the income-tax system (namely, expanding the Earned Income Tax Credit program).

The bottom line is that, for both of these reasons, making this quid-pro-quo transaction a reality will be a costly undertaking. This is particularly so since, politically, it will prove difficult over the long run to limit such benefits as expanded wage subsidies for low-wage workers, or continuing child-care provision, to only the (ex)-welfare population. Moreover, the moral question arises as to why, with general assistance benefits being cut or eliminated in some states, and with the prison populations of the various states growing rapidly, the target population for promoting the capacity and remuneration for dignified work should be limited to that segment of the low-skilled population which happens to consist of single mothers. Once the support of work for indigent and difficult-to-employ women with children has been institutionalized, how does one justify excluding from such support the brothers of these women, or the fathers of their children?

It seems to me that "work" in this workfare discussion is not really a quid-pro-quo matter at all. Recipients will not be "giving" very much in return for the benefits they receive. The transaction is "balanced" only in the sense that the recipients are seen to be making an effort. But they may be adding very little net value, once all costs of their support are taken into account, and once the opportunity costs of their time way from home (and children) are added in. What seems really to matter is that recipients are visibly trying to do something for themselves. This is what we are calling "work," in our effort to resolve the conflict between the values of self-reliance and altruism.

Toward the end of his *Atlantic Monthly* article on welfare reform, Peter Edelman observes that, in a sense, much of welfare policy is really better thought of as disability policy.[1] One-third of the welfare caseload involves some disability in either the mother or the child; between one-third and one-half of the caseload seems not to be employable, since that many remain without jobs in the best "supported work" experiments, after three years of concerted effort. A great number of these folks are socially, psychologically, physically, or mentally impaired. Young children are involved. Why is our response properly conceived along this single dimension of work?

Yet "workfare" has carried the day. Should it have? How did we end up here? The answer, I think, is neither historical inevitability nor intellectual force, but rather political expediency. This reflects poorly, I believe, on the position of progressive advocates in the contemporary political environment. Progressives found in "workfare" a salable antidote to conservative reaction against welfare policy. David Ellwood's answer to Charles Murray was "If you work hard and play by the rules, you shouldn't be poor."[2] But, where does this leave the great number of people who are not able (or willing) to "work hard and play by the rules"? Do they (and their children), then, deserve to be poor? In other words, is the distinction be-

---

[1] Peter Edelman, "The Worst Thing Bill Clinton Has Done," *Atlantic Monthly* 279.3 (March 1997).

[2] David T. Ellwood, *Poor Support* (New York: Basic Books, 1988).

tween deserving and undeserving—between "good" and "bad"—poor people a political and moral necessity in our time? And, can (or should) we make this distinction stick when the consequence is the suffering of innocent children? It is hard to avoid some such conclusions, once one has started down this path. Professor Solow does not address these questions, but his argument raises them, and they should be addressed.

So, a line of argument that began with the idea that everyone has to pull his own weight (or, in Phil Gramm's colorful and candid version: "It's time for those riding in the wagon to get out and help the rest of us push") ends with a five-year lifetime limit on receipt of federal income support for what appears to be millions of indigent families incapable of supporting themselves. This does not look like progress to me, unless you believe that enforcing this regime will set in motion a chain of forces that ultimately reduces dramatically the number of families in this position. So far as I can see, there is no reason to believe that, though only time will tell.

PROFESSOR Solow observed in his first lecture that a concern for human values could not do without economics. By this he meant that, where there are choices to be made among competing ends embodying conflicting values, an assessment of actual alternatives before us (as opposed to the ones we might wish we faced) is a prerequisite to genuinely moral action. For only by acknowledging the conflicts and constraints as they are will we be led to doing the work of moral reflection that must be done. The frequent making of this prototypical economist's observation is what has earned our profession the reputation of being the "dismal science." Yet the observation is a tautology: whatever course of action is ultimately undertaken must inevitably be constrained by the limitations of resources and information of the sort with which economics is concerned.

Yet, this tautology has a limited range of application. It does not apply, I believe, to the products of our imaginations, including our political imaginations. Indeed and perversely, if we think only about what appears to be politically feasible at a point in time, we may limit our ability to conceive of something genuinely fresh and new. I think that something like this may be the case in this area of social policy. This is why I want to think about more than the "work" question in this discussion.

The Social Security Act of 1935 was a great achievement, creating the system of income support for the elderly which is today universally embraced, across the political spectrum, as a bedrock public commitment. The 1935 act also created the federal program of assistance to families with dependent children which we commonly call welfare, and which was dramatically altered by the welfare reform legislation signed into law by President Clinton in 1996. That legislation ended the federal entitlement to assistance that poor, single-parent families had enjoyed for over sixty years. In this context, a particularly sharp issue—which must be raised here—involves the poorest of the poor, the so-called "underclass." To speak plainly and directly, I do not believe that the progressive spirit of the New Deal, as reflected in the social democratic policy arguments of many on the Left today when addressing the problem of the underclass, remains adequate in the face of the profound difficulties that we face in this area. I think those arguments need to be modified, if the objective of incorporating the socially marginalized more fully into the body politic—an objective that I share—is to be achieved.

There is a progressive "story" about the underclass that has gained wide currency. This story is reflected in the work of distinguished sociologist William Julius Wilson, whom Professor Solow has mentioned more than once during these lectures. In his new and important book, *When Work Disappears,* Wilson claims that the absence of "good jobs at good wages" in the central cities has precipitated the social collapse to be observed there; and that, until employment opportunities are restored through concerted government action, the tragic, pathological disintegration will continue apace. I want to question these claims, particularly the notion that the root cause of behavioral pathology in the ghettos is the disappearance of work. In this way, I want further to support my view that "work" is too narrow a lens through which to view the problem of what to do about the welfare population.

It is, of course, true that attachment to the workforce is extraordinarily low among residents of inner-city ghettos. It is also true that their attachments to marriage, school, and law-abidingness are extremely low, as well. Which is cause, and which effect? I do not know the answer to this question, and neither, it seems to me, does Professor Wilson, Professor Solow, or anyone else. The leading alternative explanations of the underclass problem are the incentive effects of transfer policies, and the autonomous influences of ghetto culture. Although I do not believe that the incentive effects of welfare have caused the growth of single parenthood, joblessness, and criminal participation in inner-city neighborhoods, I am not nearly so certain that the self-destructive patterns of behavior among successive generations of ghetto youths, reinforced by cultural changes throughout American society, and certainly not helped by the lack of economic opportunity, have not taken on a life of their own, substantially independent of economic trends. As such, it is unclear that the provision of (even well-supported) work opportunities will suffice to resolve these difficulties.

Here is the problem: too many young ghetto dwellers are unfit for work. They lack the traits of temperament, character, and intellect to function effectively in the workplace. They have not been socialized within families from the earliest ages to delay gratification, to exercise self-control, to communicate effectively, to embrace their responsibilities, and even in some cases to feel empathy for their fellows. These deficits are not genetic; but they are certainly exacerbated by racial and class segregation in this society, they obviously reflect the disadvantages of being born into societal backwaters, and they should elicit a sympathetic response from the rest of society. They are nevertheless deficits, deep and profound, and they may not be easily reversible with jobs programs of any kind.

Let me observe here that the opposition that some are inclined to raise in this context between structural explanations of social pathology, on the one hand, and individualistic explanations on the other is, in my opinion, a false dichotomy, a red herring, a canard. To be the only young male in a housing project environment who carries books home from school, marries the girl he gets pregnant, and works for "chump change" at a fast-food franchise, an individual would have to behave heroically. We cannot ex-

COMMENT

pect heroism as the norm. Thus, to point a finger at the individual in that circumstance who fails to measure up to our expectations, and to condemn that individual as "immoral," is callous and is itself an immoral stance. The individual is, of course, constrained by the structure in which he is imbedded. On the other hand, to ignore the extent to which environments of this sort foster patterns of behavior that are morally problematic (and also inefficacious) is to make a serious mistake, as well.

I doubt that Professor Solow would disagree with me on these points, though I am not sure about that. (We shall find out soon enough.) But, let me push this point a bit further: there is good reason to doubt that the provision of WPA-style public jobs, as Wilson advocates, or jobs oriented toward developing skills useful in the service sector, as Professor Solow advocates, will reverse the disintegration of the black family, drive crack from the ghettos or, for that matter, transform the negative attitudes toward work and responsibility that Wilson himself documents, in the quotations he presents from both young black men and their prospective employers in the first part of his book. And, if you think you can solve the ghetto problem by dealing only with women on welfare and their children, you need to think again. It is just possible that more, much more, will be needed to reverse the tragic disintegration of social life in the urban ghettos. It may be that social policy, by itself, is not capable of eradicating deeply entrenched patterns of child rearing and social interaction that pass on personal incapacity—criminal violence, promiscuous sexuality, early unwed childbearing, academic failure—from one generation to the next. It is imaginable, is it not, that the moral life of the hard core

53

urban poor will have to be transformed before some of these most marginalized souls will be able to seize such opportunity as may exist.

One can surely understand why an economist whose focus is on employment issues might hesitate to make this point. But it would be too bad if, at a convocation of the University Center for Human Values, we were to leave without having considered the point at all.

✤ COMMENT ✤

ANTHONY LEWIS

✤

Professor Solow mentioned the Peter Edelman article in the *Atlantic Monthly* describing harsh effects of the 1996 welfare legislation and criticizing President Clinton's role in it.[1] When I wrote a column about the Edelman piece, I had an angry letter from a reader in Long Island. His parents came to this country as refugees after World War Two with just $10 in their pockets. If they had been given welfare, he said, they would have "remained in a terrible state." Instead they worked hard and made it into the middle class. He concluded, in capital letters: "Welfare and food stamps are a DIABOLICAL LIBERAL INVENTION to keep a large population destitute, and to guarantee a voting bloc for politicians who promise the best handout."

That letter illustrates one of Professor Solow's starting points. We live in a society that puts a high value on self-reliance. Those who pay taxes may sorely resent supporting a welfare system that they believe saps self-reliance.

But the letter's political argument, its denunciation of the devilish liberals, proceeds from a faulty premise. Americans who receive welfare are not an effective voting

[1] Peter Edelman, "The Worst Thing Bill Clinton Has Done," *Atlantic Monthly* 279.3 (March 1997), 43.

55

bloc. Their lack of influence was evident when Congress in the 1996 legislation ended the federal guarantee of aid to poor families with dependent children. The fact is that poor people, on or off welfare, mostly do not vote in this country. The question is why those who *do* vote, better-off citizens, came to feel so strongly that the welfare system was breeding a corrupt dependency and was taking unfair advantage of the taxpayer. Why now? Why did we abandon the federal guaranty at a time when the country was at a high point of prosperity, very likely the greatest prosperity of any country, ever?

Prosperity itself is part of the answer, I think. When the first major federal social programs were enacted, in the 1930s, Americans were all too familiar with economic deprivation. Most adults had themselves been impoverished by the Depression or were close enough to people who had to empathize with the victims of poverty. The enrichment of the last fifty years—the growth of the middle class and upper middle class—has made us more likely to be Social Darwinists: to believe that the fittest survive in the market, and those who do not make it have only their own shiftlessness to blame.

But the radical nature of the legislation passed by Congress and signed into law by President Clinton, the abolition of the main federal safety net, also reflected a growing belief—across ideological lines—that the existing welfare system was fostering destructive patterns of life. Critical as he was of the 1996 law, Peter Edelman agreed that the system needed changing to encourage work instead of reliance on welfare checks. After the legislation was enacted, the *Boston Globe* did a lengthy study of welfare recipients in rural Massachusetts; a commentator concluded that they displayed these qualities: "Self-indulgence. Sloth. Amorality." People on welfare themselves expressed concern, in newspaper interviews, about what the system had done to their character. Many seemed to agree with Professor Solow's wry comment that in our society long-term reliance on others' altruism "may be dangerous to one's moral health."

Which brings me back to the Tanner Lectures. After hearing Professor Solow remark that "welfare bums were a topic of conversation at the Club in Caesarea fifteen hundred years ago," one can no longer think of economics as, necessarily, a dismal science. The wit and elegance of the lectures were matched by the clarity with which they exposed the *facts* of welfare and work. That is important, because the heated debate on the question has been astonishingly short on reliable facts.

It makes a great difference, for example, to learn that a substantial number of those now on welfare cannot work full time, no matter what incentives may be put in place. It was news to me that nearly half of current recipients either get both welfare and earnings from part-time work or else alternate working and living on welfare. And Professor Solow was unrelentingly realistic in describing the difficulty of moving some people from welfare to work. Programs in California and Michigan, he showed, increased the percentage who became employed only slightly despite serious, extended efforts. His conclusion is one that should be at the center of thinking on the welfare question: "Without some added ingredients, the transformation of welfare into work is likely to be the transformation of welfare into unemployment and casual earnings so low as once to have been thought unacceptable for fellow citizens."

The question is whether politicians will face that conclusion or go on assuming, wishfully, that welfare recipients forced by the strict new limits to look for jobs will be able to find minimally decent ones. I say wishfully because the 1996 welfare law was passed on the basis of wish and ideology rather than facts. No one who pushed it—nor the president who signed it—knows how poor children and ill adults will actually survive under its terms.

Professor Solow embraces the goal of work, not welfare—provided that the formula in application is "neither punitive nor degrading," that it is applied with care to the disabled and troubled, and that it shows concern for the needs of children. I wonder how many of those who promoted the 1996 law bore those considerations in mind. I rather think that some of them took their cue from Dickens's Mr. Bumble and Wackford Squeers. That is, they meant to be punitive. How else can one explain depriving elderly and disabled legal immigrants of food stamps and other benefits? The purpose could not have been to make them go to work, since they are unable to work.

"It is legitimate for taxpayers to want welfare recipients to work," Professor Solow says, "but not so legitimate to want them to live at the miserable standard their earning capacity can provide, least of all if children are involved." So a decent new system would provide support for earnings and create jobs for those who want to get off welfare. That would not be cheap, and Professor Solow sees no sign that our society in its present mood is prepared to put up the needed money. He is surely correct in that pessimism. The 1996 welfare law was shaped not by such rational calculations but mainly, I believe, by the desire to reduce federal responsibility and budgetary cost.

The welfare problem lies, Professor Solow says, at the intersection of two values: self-reliance and altruism. But when you think about some of the human evidence he cites, you might conclude that other values are involved, too. I was struck by the woman who said she was glad for welfare because it allowed her to stay home with her baby. "I'd love to get off welfare," she said, "but I'm not going to miss my son growing up just to get off it." Doesn't that sound like a value that all of us, regardless of ideological bent, ought to honor? Or does the Protestant work ethic trump everything else in our society?

There was one point at which I parted from Professor Solow. It was when he said that we working taxpayers tax ourselves to help the poor because of altruism—"even if," he added, "it includes an attenuated element of enlightened self-interest." No doubt there was irony in his comment, but in any event the self-interest is in my view far from attenuated. Not long ago I was walking across East Forty-Third Street in New York between Fifth and Madison Avenues. A woman came toward me, in her thirties I would say, respectably dressed, with a boy of perhaps six walking next to her and a baby in a stroller. She stopped me. "Could you spare some money?" she asked. "We've had nothing to eat today." Is that the way we want to live, we the fortunate? Some of us can wall ourselves off in guarded communities. But the quality of our lives is still deeply affected by the existence of Americans like that woman and her children, and by the existence of blighted ghettos in the centers of our cities.

I give you the example of South Africa, a country that is in both the first and the third worlds. It has suburbs as lush as any in the United States, and it has squatter settlements of tin and cardboard that go as far as the eye can see. Years ago, in the time of apartheid, a Catholic bishop said to me that most white South Africans suffered from existential blindness; they blinded themselves to the bitter realities around them so they could go on living untroubled lives. It is no longer possible to overlook the realities in South Africa. Do *we* want a society where we blind ourselves to the reality of people who are desperately poor?

Professor Solow focused on the question of welfare and work. But there is more to the problem of poverty and urban decay in this country, as I know he would agree. There is the daunting reality, so powerfully described by Professor William Julius Wilson, that large numbers of young men in the ghettos of Chicago—and elsewhere—lack the education and even the primary social skills to be employable in today's economy. They do not know how to be on time, how to apply themselves to a task until it is done.

That brings me to the unmentioned subject that underlies so much of the welfare debate: race. We had a question from the audience about the failure of Britain to respond adequately to the potato famine in Ireland. The failure is thought to have reflected, to some degree, a British feeling that the Irish were feckless people who had brought disaster upon themselves. A similar feeling among white Americans about blacks has surely contributed to the clampdown on welfare. Professor Solow referred elliptically to that when he spoke of a Canadian welfare experiment and said many Americans would dismiss it as irrelevant to us because "those are Canadians (meaning 'white people down on their luck')." In addressing any part of our social pathology we cannot escape race.

But I have strayed from Professor Solow's rational realm. Or have I?

JOHN E. ROEMER

✣

P ROFESSOR SOLOW's lucid and sensitive presentation is a hard act to follow. I have little to criticize in his analysis, and shall therefore concentrate my attention on things he only touched upon, or left unsaid. In particular, I shall try to evaluate, in a broad-brush way, the economic and political feasibility of one of the two alternatives to "welfare as we know it" that he referred to, an employer subsidy program; and I shall then offer a few remarks on equality of opportunity.

First, then, to an analysis of what employer subsidies could do. I must preface these remarks by reminding you that I am not a labor economist, and so I am innocent of much of the detail of how labor markets work—in particular, how their actual working differs from the textbook picture of markets. What I shall offer you is a standard, textbook analysis of employer subsidy programs, and that analysis may be open to critique on grounds that actual labor markets do not operate as they are generally conceived of as operating. But bear in mind that, in the following analysis, markets are assumed to be perfect, and it is assumed that the economy would flexibly adapt to the influx of new labor from those currently on welfare. Thus, the projections I make err on the optimistic side.

I shall try to imitate Professor Solow's admirably non-technical description of an economic model. In the model I construct to study employer subsidies, I assume there are two kinds of worker, high-skill and low-skill. The single consumption good in the economy is produced by high- and low-skill labor, who cooperate in the production process. I have used what is called a CES production function to capture exactly how the two kinds of labor combine to produce output. In the model, all high-skill labor is employed, but there is generally some unemployment of low-skill labor, and this is due to the fact that low-skill workers face costs, in varying amounts, if they go to work. Think of these costs as those of child care: if one stays at home, one can take care of the children, but if one goes to work, someone else must be paid to do so. A low-skill worker will seek employment only if her after-tax wage earnings exceed the welfare benefit she receives if unemployed by at least these costs. Economists often refer to such costs as the disutility of labor, but I think it is more apposite to think of them as child-care expenses. High-skill workers also have such costs, but their wages will always be high enough to make it worthwhile to work, rather than to stay home and collect the transfer payment. In any event, I assume that there is a given distribution of these costs of working among the population of low-skill citizens.

Citizens must tax themselves to raise funds to pay benefits to the unemployed, here conceived of as the welfare benefit. We can now describe the market equilibrium of such an economy, without employer subsidies. In fact, for each possible level of the welfare benefit, there will be an equilibrium, consisting of a pair of wages, one for low-skill and the other for high-skill workers, and a proportional income tax levied on the incomes of all employed workers. Firms in the economy are competitive, and maximize profits. At equilibrium for a given value of the welfare benefit, the two wages are such that the demand for high-skill labor by firms exactly equals the total supply of high-skill workers in the economy, and the demand for low-skill workers by firms exactly equals the amount of low-skill labor on offer, which is the total labor supply of low-skill workers for whom it is profitable to offer labor, that is, for whom after-tax income will exceed the welfare benefit by at least their child-care costs. Further, the income tax just suffices to pay total welfare benefits.

To refer to Professor Solow's exposition, this is an economy where those on welfare are exact substitutes in production for employed low-skill labor. Furthermore, employment will always expand to accommodate a larger supply of low-skill labor, but at the same time, the wage of low-skill labor will fall. The model is neoclassical.

I have to calibrate this model so that it looks something like the U.S. economy: of course, since the model only has a few parameters, and the U.S. economy has millions of parameters, I cannot exactly capture what our economy looks like in its salient features. The inexactness of the picture that you will see in a minute is the opportunity cost of model simplicity.

I calibrated the model so that if all labor is fully employed then average income is $40,000, which was approximately average household income in the United States a few years ago. At this full-employment equilibrium, the wage of low-skill workers is $13,400 and the high-skill wage is $58,000. (Remember, everyone other than our low-skill population is lumped into one kind of labor, here designated "high-skill.") For the economists in the audience, I chose the elasticity of substitution between the two kinds of labor to be 1.5, as the conventional wisdom has it that that elasticity is between one and two.

I further calibrate the model by assuming that 40 percent of the population is low-skill, and 60 percent is high-skill, and that among low-skill workers there is a uniform distribution of child-care costs varying between none and $20,000. It is people at the high end of this cost continuum who will almost always be on welfare.

In table 1, I report the various equilibria that are available to us, as we vary the welfare benefit—this is "welfare as we know it," with no employer subsidies or jobs program. The first column, *lam*, lists the employment rate of low-skill labor; the second column, *tax*, the proportional income tax rate; *bene* is the welfare benefit (in $1000s), *lowage* is the after-tax wage of low-skill workers, *hiwage* is the after-tax wage of high-skill workers, *mean* is average income in economy, meaning per capita GNP, and *gini* is the gini coefficient of the income distribution, among the three classes—high-skill workers, low-skill employed workers, and low-skill workers collecting the benefit. Consider the fifth row of the table. The employment rate of low-skill workers is 60 percent, which translates into a gross unemployment rate of 16 percent. (Recall, this does not use the standard definition of the labor force, but rather takes the denominator in the unemployment rate as the entire adult population.) The welfare benefit is $5,700, and the after-tax wage of low-skill workers is $17,700. (Thus, those collecting welfare are precisely the individuals for whom child-care costs exceed $12,000.)

TABLE 1 Zero Employer Subsidy

lam	tax	bene	lowage	hiwage	mean	gini
0.8	−0.00135904	−0.663805	15.3362	57.0341	39.0749	0.28624
0.75	0.0022463	0.870728	15.8707	56.5242	38.7628	0.28653
0.7	0.00761509	2.43926	16.4393	55.9042	38.4382	0.28487
0.65	0.014876	4.04835	17.0484	55.1672	38.0997	0.28120
0.6	0.0241889	5.70635	17.7064	54.3046	37.7453	0.27543
0.55	0.0357563	7.42401	18.424	53.3057	37.373	0.26744
0.5	0.0498403	9.21547	19.2155	52.1564	36.98	0.25705
0.45	0.0667877	11.0997	20.0997	50.8381	36.5628	0.24400
0.4	0.087072	13.132	21.1032	49.3258	36.1167	0.22794

Note, from the second column, that the welfare program costs 2.4 percent of GNP.

How could we raise the participation rate in the labor force of low-skill workers from 60 percent to 80 percent? The negative numbers in the first row of the table tell us that this is impossible. Even to raise the participation rate to 75 percent, we would have to lower the welfare benefit to $870 (per annum). By inducing that extra 15 percent into the labor force, we would lower the after-tax earnings of employed low-skill workers from $17,700 to $15,870—that is, by 10 percent. This nontrivial reduction in income is the cost of increasing labor-force participation to the so-called "deserving poor" that Professor Solow referred to. Notice also that the income distribution would become more unequal, as measured by an increase in gini coefficient from 0.275 to 0.287. GNP per capita would rise by a mere 2.7 percent.

It is also instructive to observe the trade-offs of going in the other direction. Suppose we wanted to raise the welfare benefit to $9,200—not a princely sum. This would entail a labor-force participation rate among low-skill workers of 50 percent. In addition, the after-tax income of the low-skill unemployed would increase to $19,200, that is, by 8.5 percent. Moreover, the gini coefficient would fall to 0.257. The cost of this change is borne by high-skill workers, whose income would decrease from $54,300 to $52,160, a decrease of 3.9 percent. You might find this an acceptable cost, but remember that high-skill workers comprise 60 percent of the polity, and they would not be happy with that reduction in real income. So the political implementation of such a regime is unlikely. No one is talking about *that* kind of welfare reform.

In figure 1, I graph for you the last two columns of the table, per capita GNP against the gini coefficient. That the curve has a positive slope is the form the efficiency-equality trade-off takes in this economy: that is, higher per capita GNP is purchased at the cost of increased inequality.

Let us now turn to a model in which firms are subsidized by the government to hire low-skill workers (table 2). We have a choice: should the subsidy be targeted to the hiring of workers currently on welfare who enter the labor force, or should firms receive the subsidy for every low-skill worker they hire? There is a debate on this issue among labor economists, which I can not discuss here. I have chosen to model the regime where the subsidy is not targeted. The main reason is that targeting the subsidy—that is, attaching it only to workers who leave welfare to take a job—would induce a deleterious substitution by firms of current low-skill welfare recipients for currently employed low-skill workers. Thus, the cost to the so-called deserving poor would be even greater than other-

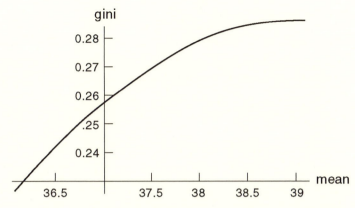

FIGURE 1. Social welfare indicators under the present system.

wise. Further, any program with targeted subsidies will require more government monitoring, and will be less politically viable.

Table 3 reports the alternatives available if we fund a 30 percent employer subsidy. Taxes now finance both the employer subsidy and the welfare benefit for those who remain unemployed. Under this regime, we can increase the

TABLE 2 15 Percent Employer Subsidy

lam	tax	bene	lowage	hiwage	mean	gini
0.8	0.0248015	1.57122	17.5712	55.5441	39.0749	0.263368
0.75	0.0292566	3.16599	18.166	54.994	38.7628	0.262848
0.7	0.0355129	4.79661	18.7966	54.3326	38.4382	0.260341
0.65	0.0437043	6.46994	19.4699	53.5528	38.0997	0.255779
0.6	0.0539975	8.19466	20.1947	52.6458	37.7453	0.249066
0.55	0.0666027	9.98191	20.9819	51.6004	37.373	0.240067
0.5	0.0817911	11.8462	21.8462	50.4025	36.98	0.228597
0.45	0.0999207	13.8072	22.8072	49.0332	36.5628	0.214388
0.4	0.121478	15.8916	23.8916	47.4668	36.1167	0.197063

TABLE 3 30 Percent Employer Subsidy

lam	tax	bene	lowage	hiwage	mean	gini
0.8	0.0598878	4.56882	20.5688	53.5457	39.0749	0.232682
0.75	0.0654004	6.23739	21.2374	52.9464	38.7628	0.231154
0.7	0.072751	7.94322	21.9432	52.2349	38.4382	0.227596
0.65	0.0820783	9.69337	22.6934	51.4038	38.0997	0.221937
0.6	0.0935543	11.4967	23.4967	50.4444	37.7453	0.214073
0.55	0.107395	13.3646	24.3646	49.3453	37.373	0.203863
0.5	0.123879	15.3117	25.3117	48.0922	36.98	0.191112
0.45	0.143369	17.3576	26.3576	46.6662	36.5628	0.175547
0.4	0.16636	19.5291	27.5291	45.0418	36.1167	0.156777

labor-force participation rate of low-skill workers to 80 percent, and still support those who remain on welfare with a benefit of $4,570, a "mere" 20 percent reduction in the benefit. Continuing the comparison to my chosen benchmark of 60 percent labor-force participation under the current regime, the post-tax income of low-skill employed workers would rise substantially from $17,700 to $20,570. But the post-tax income of high-skill workers would fall from $54,300 to $53,550, by 1.4 percent. You might think this is a worthwhile trade-off, but it is not obvious that the median voter would agree. A socially better alternative, I think, would be to move to a 75 percent participation rate under the 30 percent employer subsidy scheme. This could be accomplished while raising the welfare benefit to $6,240 (from $5,700), increasing the after-tax earnings of the working low-skilled to $21,200, and reducing the after-tax earnings of the high-skilled to $52,950, a reduction of 2.5 percent. Again, we must confront the self-interest of the median voter. And note that we are talking about a rather small increment of 15 to 20 percent, in the labor-force participation rate of low-skill workers.

Although rational, self-interested economic agents will only look at what happens to their after-tax incomes, we should note that to achieve a 75 percent participation rate with the 30 percent employer subsidy program would cost 6.5 percent of GNP, in contrast to the 2.4 percent fraction of GNP in the benchmark of 60 percent participation rate of "welfare as we know it." This verifies Professor Solow's claim that a successful program will be much more expensive than what we now have.

Finally, figure 2 presents the aggregate welfare economics of three regimes, in which the top curve is the present system, the middle curve is a 15 percent employer subsidy program, and the bottom curve is the 30 percent employer subsidy program. The lower the curve is, the better is the regime from the aggregate welfare viewpoint, at least according to my ethics: that is, on a lower curve, we can generate the same GNP per capita with a more equal distribution of income than on a higher curve. So, from an aggregate welfare viewpoint, the 30 percent employer subsidy program is the best. What we have seen, however, is that a move from what we have at present to a more desirable equilibrium with an employer subsidy program would not be in the self-interest of the median voter, the high-skill worker. Political economy confronts welfare economics.

Let me turn, now, to equality of opportunity. Professor Solow has addressed himself, in these lectures, to a short-run problem: how to get those low-skill workers, currently not participating in the labor force, into the labor force. As I hope my calculations have indicated, the

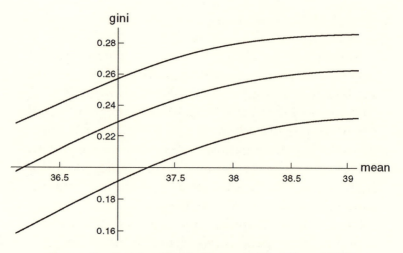

FIGURE 2.   Social welfare indicators at 0%, 15%, and 30%
employer subsidies.

prospects for doing so in our market economy are not aus-
picious, even with a wage-subsidy program. I have not
analyzed a jobs program. The longer-run solution to the
problem must, I think, involve increasing the skills of low-
skill workers. Assuming that the technology would adjust
to accommodate a labor force with a better distribution of
skills, then real wages for all workers would increase, and
fewer low-skill workers would find it advantageous to remain out of the labor force. I agree with Professor Solow
that almost all people would like to work, if they could do
so and not lose financially, given what I've called their
child-care costs.

There are two general approaches to increasing the
skills of the disadvantaged: one is through better primary
and secondary education, the other is through post-school
job training. I guess the most successful institution, in our

country, that does the latter is the military, which perhaps explains why so many poorly educated people find the military attractive.

Not to the exclusion of more post-school skill enhancement programs, I advocate a substantial increase in what we spend on primary and secondary education. Implementing such an increase in a democracy requires convincing citizens to tax themselves at a higher rate, and this observation is enough to end the discussion among political sophisticates. The basis for a cautious optimism is the expressed belief, by the vast majority of American citizens, in policies that guarantee equal opportunity. The salient question is what equal opportunity requires.

I would like briefly to articulate the view that equalizing opportunity means leveling the playing field. Let us be specific here, and ask what would be required to equalize opportunity for future earning capacity among the nation's children. What are the troughs and mounds in the playing field that, at present, inhibit the equalization of that kind of opportunity? I say they are the circumstances, beyond the control of individual children, that either give them a head start, or restrain them, in the process of preparing themselves to be productive adults. Among these, the most important is the socio-economic status of the family. Children from low SES families acquire, on average, lower adult earning capacity than children from high SES families. It is important to note that I do not deny that, within the cohort of children from families of a given socio-economic status, there will be a large range of adult earning capacities acquired, and this is because there are other circumstances than SES that are important; and in addition to circumstances, there is effort—which I take to

be hard work exercised in virtue of autonomous voli-
tion—that is differentially applied among any group of
people with roughly equal sets of circumstances.

An equal-opportunity-for-adult-earning-capacities policy should, I claim, compensate those in unfortunate circumstances with additional resources, so that their distribution of acquired earning capacities is as similar as
possible to the distribution of acquired earning capacities
of those in more advantageous circumstances. Equal opportunity for adult earning capacity will have been
achieved when expected adult earnings depend only on
one's effort, not on one's circumstances.

Concretely, what would such a policy mean in regard to
public education? It would mean spending a good deal
more on the education of children from disadvantageous
circumstances than on children from advantaged back-
grounds. Contrary to one popular view, it would *not* mean
equal educational expenditures on all children—although
that equal resource allocation would be an improvement
over what we have now in the United States, in most
places.

The skeptic should, at this point, march out the median
voter to prove the utopian essence of my proposal. Why
should the median voter agree to this kind of compensatory educational spending and, moreover, to an increase
in the aggregate education budget, less reluctantly than
she would agree to lower her real wage in order to increase the labor-force participation rate of low-skill workers, in the model I discussed earlier? I certainly cannot
confidently respond that she would, but I do think there
is a basis for some hope, due to the commitment, among
Americans to equal opportunity. I am proposing a plausi-

ble interpretation of that concept, which, if generally accepted, would induce citizens to advocate the kind of public policy, in respect of educational finance, that I have described. A first step is to win over our social scientists and philosophers to advocate this view—hence, these words.

APPENDIX

In the model of the comment, it is assumed that the production function is

$$y = \alpha \, (\gamma L_1^{\rho} + (1 - \gamma)L_2^{\rho})^{1/\rho}$$

where L_1 is low-skill labor and L_2 is high-skill labor. Fraction σ of workers are high-skill, and fraction β are low-skill, where $\sigma + \beta = 1$. Let λ be the employment rate of low-skill workers, let p be the fraction of low-skill wage that is subsidized by the government, and let $w_1 (w_2)$ be the low-skill (high-skill) wage. Let b be the welfare benefit paid to each unemployed low-skill worker, and let F be the C.D.F. of the "child-care costs" of low-skill workers, defined on a support $[0,a]$. Then an equilibrium at tax rate t and subsidy rate p is a vector $(w_1, w_2, \lambda, b, \delta^*)$ satisfying the following five equations:
The utility function of an unskilled worker is given by:

$$\alpha\gamma(\gamma + (1 - \gamma)(\frac{\sigma}{\lambda\beta})^{\rho})^{\frac{1-\rho}{\rho}} = (1 - p)w_1 \tag{1}$$

$$\alpha(1 - \gamma)(\gamma - (1 - \gamma)(\frac{\sigma}{\lambda\beta})^{\rho})^{\frac{1-\rho}{\rho}}(\frac{\sigma}{\lambda\beta})^{\rho-1} = w_2 \tag{2}$$

$$t\sigma\omega_2 + t\lambda\beta w_1 = b(1 - \lambda)\beta + pw_1\lambda\beta \tag{3}$$

$$\lambda = F(\delta^*) \tag{4}$$

$$\delta^* = (1-t)w_1 - b. \tag{5}$$

The utility function of an unskilled worker is given by:

post-tax income $- \delta$, if working

welfare benefit b, if not working,

where δ is her child-care cost.

Equations (1) and (2) come from profit maximization and clearing of the two labor markets; equation (3) is the balanced-budget equation; equation (4) says that employed low-skill workers are precisely those whose child-care costs are less than δ^*, and equation (5) says δ^* is the excess of the post-tax low-skill wage over the welfare benefit.

I chose $\beta = 0.4$, $\sigma = 0.6$, $\gamma = 0.15$, and $\rho = 0.33$, and then computed $\alpha = 71$, to generate GNP per capita at full employment of 40. Thus the elasticity of substitution is $1/(1-\rho) = 1.5$. I chose F to be the uniform distribution on the interval $[0, 20]$.

The gini coefficient is computed for the discrete income distribution with three income levels of b, $(1-t)w_1$, and $(1-t)w_2$ for the three classes. Tables 1, 2, and 3 report various equilibria for $p = 0$, 0.15, and 0.30, respectively.

GERTRUDE HIMMELFARB

✣

IF PROFESSOR SOLOW'S colleagues find the theme of his lecture, economics and human values, oxymoronic, it can only be because they have strayed so far from their roots. Adam Smith, they might recall, held the chair not of Political Economy but of Moral Philosophy, and established his reputation, long before *The Wealth of Nations*, with *The Theory of Moral Sentiments;* indeed, his last work before his death was the preparation of the sixth edition of *Moral Sentiments.* And when Smith's friend Edmund Burke made that famous statement, "The age of chivalry is gone, that of sophisters, economists, and calculators has succeeded," it was because he was beginning to see the rise of a new economics that was not in the humanistic tradition of Smith.

More than a century later, the economist Alfred Marshall returned to that earlier tradition. As if in direct refutation of Burke, he declared, "The age of chivalry is not over." In an essay "The Social Possibilities of Economic Chivalry," he described the "latent chivalry" in business. Just as medieval chivalry had mitigated the horrors of warfare, so economic chivalry would mitigate the excesses of commercial competition. As medieval chivalry had elicited an unselfish loyalty to prince and kingdom, so economic chivalry would cultivate a spirit of public service. And as medieval chivalry put a knight's courage and endurance to the test, so economic chivalry would induce an entrepreneur to take "a delight in doing noble and difficult things because they are noble and difficult."

Marshall's "chivalry" resembles Solow's "altruism," one of the "building blocks" of the welfare system. Indeed, all of Solow's building blocks are preeminently Victorian. Solow finds in the late Roman empire premonitions of the modern welfare state. But the Victorians, even more than the ancient Romans whom he cites, have much to teach us about the relationship of economics to human values—not, however, as a precedent for the welfare state but as an alternative to it.

The first of these building blocks, "a real, but limited, supply of altruism," perfectly describes late-Victorian England, which witnessed an unprecedented surge of philanthropic activities. It was "real" altruism—the only effective kind of altruism, the Victorians insisted—because it was not checkbook charity but depended upon the personal involvement of the benefactors, a giving of themselves as well as of their money. And it was "limited," in the sense that it was not "indiscriminate": charity was to be given to those who could benefit from it and in such forms as would be most beneficial to them.

Another of Solow's building blocks, "the internalized social norm that values self-reliance," is more familiarly known as the Puritan ethic, which the Victorians, even more perhaps than the Puritans, valued so highly. It is also known as the work ethic, an ethic that makes a virtue of all those qualities associated with work: responsibility, temperance, prudence, self-discipline, and, above all, self-reliance—or, as the Victorians put it, "independence." (A common term for the working classes, the laboring poor, was the "independent poor.")

It is only in the last few decades that we in the United States have started to worry about the "culture of dependency," a culture in which welfare replaces work as the normal, acceptable way of life, not for individuals alone but for entire communities and successive generations. The Victorians worried about it all the time, and made it a prime goal of social policy to deter such dependency by encouraging individuals to internalize those virtues that promoted independence, thus enabling them to police themselves, as it were. This was a prime tenet of Victorian liberalism: the more effective the internal exercise of morality, the less need there would be for the external, coercive instruments of the state.

But the Victorians, even the most liberal and laissez-faire of them, did not presume to do without the state entirely. Which brings us to the third of Solow's building blocks: a welfare system intended to serve the class "whose earning power is at best inadequate to support a minimally respectable standard of life." Here too, Victorian England has much to tell us, for its system of welfare—not a welfare state but relief in the context of a liberal state—went through a period of crisis and reform not unlike that which we are now experiencing.

ENGLAND has always had, alongside its flourishing system of private charities, a long and well-established system of public relief. The English poor laws, dating back to Elizabethan times, gave England the distinction of being the first country to establish a compulsory, secular, national (although locally administered) system of relief. At different times and in different localities, that system expanded or contracted, depending upon economic circumstances and the social temper.

The late eighteenth and early nineteenth centuries were a period of expansion, largely as the result of a new policy known as the Speenhamland System, which provided relief not only to the indigent ("paupers," as they were known) but to farm laborers whose earnings fell below a minimal standard determined by the price of bread and the size of the family. That provision (a family allowance, in effect) led to a vast increase in the number of those receiving relief, a substantial rise in the poor rates (the taxes levied to pay for that relief), serious dislocations in the economy (a decline of the yeomanry, a fall in productivity, higher food prices, and so on), all of which had ripple effects throughout the industrial as well as agricultural sector. But what troubled contemporaries most was the effect on the poor themselves—the "pauperization" and "demoralization" not only of the pauper class but of those of the laboring poor who were reduced to the psychological and social status of paupers.

In 1834 a royal commission appointed to inquire into the poor laws produced a remarkably shrewd and sophisticated report. The problem, it said, was "the mischievous ambiguity of the word *poor*"—the blurring of the distinction between pauper and poor, between the indigent and the independent laboring poor. And it proposed to eliminate that ambiguity not by abolishing the poor laws, as Malthus and others suggested, but by reforming them. Those historians who see the report, and the New Poor Law inspired by it, as simply regressive or reactionary ignore the basic feature of the reform: the perpetuation of the institution of poor relief and the reaffirmation of the right to relief.

Indeed, one class of paupers was unaffected by the reform. The "impotent" (the aged and infirm, orphans and widows with young children) would continue to receive "outdoor relief" (the dole) or, if they were homeless, would be cared for in poorhouses. It was the "able-bodied" who were regarded as the problem, and it was for them that the reform was intended. They too would receive relief (anything else, the report said, would be "repugnant to the common sentiments of mankind"), but they would do so in accord with the principle of "less eligibility": The requirement that their living conditions be less "eligible" (that is, less desirable or favorable) than those of the independent laborer. And less eligibility meant, among other things, that the able-bodied should get relief only within the workhouse.

The workhouse was not a new institution; it was as old as the poor laws themselves. What was new was the use of the workhouse to implement the principle of less eligibility by preserving the distinction between the able-bodied pauper and the independent laborer, so that the latter would not be tempted into a state of pauperism. In fact, the New Poor Law of 1834 was less rigorous in its provisions, and even less so in its implementation, than the report. Many parishes continued to provide outdoor relief for the able-bodied, and the conditions in the new workhouses were often better than those of some laborers eking out a bare subsistence in their cottages. But the idea of the workhouse became the symbol and stigma of pauperism, and in this sense the ultimate deterrent to pauperism. For the able-bodied pauper it was a powerful inducement to find work. And for the laborer it was a powerful inducement to remain independent.

The reformers were entirely conscious of what they were doing. They wanted to encourage independence and discourage dependency, for economic reasons (to reduce the burden of taxation, create a productive labor force, and further economic growth) and for social and moral reasons: to prevent the pauperization and demoralization of the poor and to promote those virtues that would make them free, responsible citizens. In this respect the reformers were not only avowedly moralistic; they were also eminently democratic. The virtues they hoped to instil in the poor were those they valued for themselves and their own families. And they gave the poor credit for being willing and able to sustain those virtues.

In recent decades, we have witnessed a deliberate, conscious effort to create a system of welfare (no longer called relief) that is "value-free," that eschews all moral distinctions and judgments by providing welfare as a matter of right, with no sanctions and no stigma attached to it. (And no principle of less eligibility, so that the working poor sometimes find themselves in a less advantageous position than those on welfare.) We have done this for the most commendable motives. We thought that we were "moralizing" the recipients of relief, assuring them the moral status of all citizens. Instead we are now discovering that we have all too often "demoralized" them—in both senses of that word: lowered their morale and weakened their moral will.

The current welfare reform is one step toward reversing

this process. In devolving welfare to the states, the national government, while continuing to fund welfare, no
longer does so as a legal entitlement. And the states, by attaching conditions to welfare—work provisions, or time
limits, or the denial of allowances for additional children
born out of wedlock, or the requirement that teenage single mothers live with their parents—are sending important moral messages to the poor and to society at large.
These are not the Victorian sanctions, to be sure; in this respect, as in so many others, we have left the Victorians
well behind us. But in the current culture, in our time and
place, they are sanctions nonetheless.

It is interesting to read interviews with mothers on welfare (Solow quotes from some of them) who, even before
the new reforms were implemented, have begun to anticipate them, going off the relief rolls of their own accord, in
some cases preferring to work even when they are left
with a net income lower than that which they would have
received from welfare. They speak of the pride, the satisfaction, the sense of worthiness they get from working
and being self-supporting. In effect, they are beginning
to internalize those social norms that are reflected in the
new law.

After years of trying to divorce social policy from
morality, we are discovering that the two are intimately
related, that there is no such thing as "value-free" policies.
All policies are value-ridden, the difference being in the
values they promote. We are also discovering that the current system of welfare is not a purely economic problem—
perhaps not primarily an economic problem. We are a rich
country and a compassionate country. We can afford to
sustain a large welfare population if we think it necessary

and desirable. What we cannot afford is a large demoralized population, a population that exhibits the social pathology associated with chronic dependency.

In the new era we are entering, legislators and policy makers—even economists—will be obliged to be moralists as well. Solow tells us that "a concern for human values cannot do without economics." That is quite true. But it is also true that a concern for economics cannot do without human values. And a concern for the poor, a genuinely compassionate concern, can no longer tolerate a system of welfare that consigns them to a culture of dependency and degrades those it professes to help. The challenge to economists is not to create a system of "workfare" that is yet another mode of welfare, but to provide incentives—economic and moral—that will revive the work ethic and stimulate the spirit of independence.

ROBERT M. SOLOW

❖

I<small>T IS A PLEASURE</small> to thank my four commentators for their courtesy and, even more, for the relevance and seriousness of their thoughts. It is all too easy, in these circumstances, to ignore what the benighted lecturer has said and pursue one's own, much more interesting, ideas. My colleagues have resisted the temptation. I think it will make for clarity if I return the favor and reply to each of them in turn, instead of trying to restate my arguments in a way that takes account of theirs.

A<small>NTHONY</small> L<small>EWIS</small> and I are pretty clearly on the same general wavelength (which comes as no surprise to either of us). He is probably right to suggest that what I called altruism may often contain a large dose of enlightened self-interest, in the special form of a wish not to live in the sort of society that forces the well-off to face, physically, the existence of extreme and unnecessary poverty. There may even be a little bit of guilt mixed into those complicated attitudes.

But then one has to answer precisely the question he raises. Why did those attitudes change in the 1980s and 1990s? Did Americans just run out of altruism, or enlightened self-interest, or guilt? I think it is over-simple to suggest that the prosperity of the past fifty years has turned us into Social Darwinists. It could have gone the other way; one might just as plausibly have expected that assured prosperity would lead to a more generous altruism. What biased the actual outcome in the other direction? It is possible that the welfare state, as it actually developed, undermined self-reliance enough to undermine itself.

At the start I want to agree that Mr. Lewis is right to emphasize the vast importance of race and racism in the argument about welfare. It is much easier to feel comfortable, not to say righteous, about having the poor always with us if they are different. Attitudes would certainly be modified if the standard image of a welfare recipient were an uneducated white mother, although the case of the Canadians suggests that the modification would not be complete. I hinted at the race factor, of course, but I left it tangential for the pedestrian reason that it led away from the labor-market implications that I felt more competent to discuss. There may be something here that explains the change of heart in the 1990s.

To come back to Mr. Lewis's questions about the sort of society "we" want, perhaps I should have followed up a more general line of thought. I mentioned that the natural setting for a "theory" of welfare is a society in which there is a bulky lower tail of people with miserably low earning capacity. It is intrinsically difficult for a "pure" market economy to deal with that situation without offending democratic ideals. It can segregate the poor out of sight—physically or morally—or it can remediate at great expense, if it knows how, or it can subsidize. Then we are back to work and welfare.

AT THE BEGINNING of my first lecture I made some teasing remarks about the trained incapacity of my professional colleagues to get mixed up with moral issues. Professor Himmelfarb quite properly embroiders on those remarks. I am amused at my own reaction to her comments; I feel the urge to defend my colleagues, a little. Most economists, at least those who know *anything* about the history of their subject, know that Adam Smith was the author of *The Theory of Moral Sentiments.* They are just a lot more interested in the Adam Smith who had the insight that the market mechanism could create order, and efficient order, out of the uncoordinated actions of greedy people. That was a remarkable thought, but it left a whole lot of work for sophisters, economists, and calculators to do. It took a century (Walras, Pareto) to get a logically coherent picture of how a complete system of competitive markets functions, and a century more (Arrow, Debreu, many others) to get a rigorous understanding of the limited reach of the Invisible Hand. We are still trying to understand the implications when some markets (like those for future goods and for some forms of insurance) are just absent. There is a lot to be said for the kind of rigor in those matters that Adam Smith could never have achieved (though I still think a little more attention to human values would help). Without it, inexpert people utter a lot of nonsense about the "market economy."

Alfred Marshall was a great economist and, like a good Victorian, happy to moralize. Elsewhere I have quoted at length his comments on the propensity of workers to seek and employers to offer fairness in wage determination. On that subject I think he had interesting and, even now, useful things to say. The passage on economic chivalry, however, seems to me to border on the fatuous. Here Professor Himmelfarb forgets Smith's tart comment that merchants rarely gather to discuss the common good without ending in a conspiracy against the public. Entrepreneurs have complex motives, just like other people; but the very competition that drives the Invisible Hand gives them little leeway for acts of chivalry.

Professor Himmelfarb provides a knowledgeable and sympathetic picture of the Victorians' approach to social policy. I can not question her characterization of the nature and intent of the Victorians' attitude toward the relief of poverty. There are two aspects of it, however, that leave me puzzled about the implications to be drawn, especially since Professor Himmelfarb seems generally to approve of the Victorian cast of mind, and to wish that our own were more like it.

The first question is: what did they contemplate for those hard-working "independent" souls who could not find jobs, through no fault of their own, or whose earning power was so low as to leave them and their children in abject, stultifying poverty? If the answer is that they were to be left to private charity, then I have to say that I much prefer some collective provision. I cannot see that taking alms from the well-off is any less damaging to "independence" than is a wage supplement from the state, or even the dole. If anything, I would guess that the psychological-sociological balance favors the state. Servility and gratitude toward one's "betters" is not my idea of propriety in a democracy. A citizen's right, even if sometimes abused, is better. A claim on private charity can also be abused, by both parties.

Second, does Professor Himmelfarb really approve of the idea of stigmatizing and oppressing paupers whose destitution arises from disability, superannuation, or mental inadequacy, and is thus not of their own making? She seems to say that the cultivation of this sort of distaste is necessary to make pauper status unattractive to low-wage workers who could otherwise simulate eligibility for outdoor relief—alas, you can not make an omelet without breaking eggs. That sort of response strikes me as far too harsh to stand as a valid solution. It seems ugly in the Victorians. It might be even worse in us both because we are richer and because it would give more scope to the racism that is often, as Mr. Lewis observed, just below (or just above) the surface of our politics. (There were some highly placed Victorians, including some economists, who were prepared to let the Irish starve during the Famine, for their own moral good. Would they have felt quite the same way if the hungry had been Protestant Englishmen?) As I hope I have made clear, I think that one must take seriously the possibility that reliance on welfare may erode some moral virtues. But the equanimity, not to say the enthusiasm, with which the Gingriches of the world propose to sacrifice children in order to punish their mothers seems way out of proportion.

PROFESSOR LOURY makes a very important point that I want to acknowledge and endorse. I argued that the successful transformation of welfare into work would require a deliberate, sustained, and costly effort to create an adequate number of the sorts of jobs that potential welfare recipients could get and hold. Professor Loury says that I understate the problem because, if that could be accomplished, there would be no excuse for excluding other hard-to-employ workers, mostly male, from the same treatment. That strikes me as quite right and significant. My focus was on the narrower issue of the reform of AFDC, and I overlooked the broader implication, which only strengthens the basic argument.

It does not bother me that the net value of the contribution of these marginal workers is likely to be small or even negative. In the first place, if the alternative is welfare then the costs of support would be paid out anyway and should not be subtracted from the gross value of the work done. In the second place, I think that the participants prefer work to welfare, feel better about themselves when they are working, and that preference should be respected. It comes from living in a culture in which self-respect as well as the respect of others is often associated with a job. Even rich people often pretend to work.

Of course any new system will have to be administered with care and humanity. I do not think I neglected the need to pay special attention to the lives of children, but I am glad to have Professor Loury add his voice. I think he is unfair to David Ellwood, however. The very notion of "working hard and playing by the rules" must automatically be interpreted to include the modifier "to the extent one can." It only takes a little bit of humanity to recognize disability when one sees it. Yes, there is sometimes a fine line between disability and malingering, but that problem is not limited to poor people. If Professor Loury thinks that any institutional repair job, workfare or other, leads inevitably to distinctions about "good" and "bad" poor people, then I disagree with him about the facts. About the principles, his quarrel is with Professor Himmelfarb, not with me, because I do not disagree.

Finally I come to the hard problem that is Professor Loury's main message. He thinks that the moral and social pathology of the urban ghetto has taken on a life of its own. I do not need to repeat the details, because he has stated them eloquently. In his view, the notion that any sort of jobs program will reverse this sort of anomie is either a naive error or a stale social-democratic slogan. All this talk about work is at best a diversion. Somehow we will have to transform the moral life of the ghetto directly. He wonders if I will disagree with him.

The one-word answer is No, but one word is not nearly enough. Habits of thought and affect and behavior, however they arise, can certainly acquire a stubborn autonomy. Changing those habits is a very complicated matter. But I do not think that I ever suggested that the mere provision of employment opportunities would be a sufficient solution at this stage of the game. From this point of view it does not matter if a failure of employment opportunities had been the precipitating cause of the disintegration of the ghetto. But I hope I suggested—because I believe it—that "in our culture" attachment to a respectable job is a necessary part of any solution to the problem of the "truly disadvantaged." In a society that values self-reliance and attaches personal identity in large part to what one "does," direct appeals for moral regeneration are unlikely to have much effect unless they come with an opportunity to live the sort of life that the society regards as worthy of respect. And a little purchasing power will do no harm either. So the availability of jobs is absolutely essential. The content of my two lectures reflects the fact that I came to them from the side of welfare reform. The relation to the much broader issue is as I have just stated. Perhaps I should add that I think Professor Loury is right when he insists that the approach from the welfare side risks leaving out of account the lives of young ghetto males. That was not on my agenda, but it had better be on someone's agenda.

Professor Loury hints at a chicken-egg problem. He says that it will do no good to offer jobs to people who have become unfit for work. I say that it will do no good to tell the same people that they should become fit for work when there are no jobs to be had. Both of those assertions can be correct, exactly as with the original chicken-and-egg. But that only implies the need for a combined strategy; and that only reinforces my conclusion that we have not yet demonstrated any real intention to attack the problem.

IMAGINE that you were a native speaker of Old Norse on temporary assignment in central New Jersey. All of a sudden, across a crowded room, you hear the unmistakable accents of someone speaking Old Norse. It sounds beautiful. That is how I feel about Professor Roemer's intervention. He is speaking my language, doing what I do in real life. A careful reader will understand the usefulness of a simple model. With only a little data, it can give you an idea of which aspects of the underlying situation matter a lot for the end result; it can even draw your attention to things you might overlook, like the need for some altruism on the part of the median voter. It is like looking at a map of an area you have only walked through.

Professor Roemer's model picks out one of the difficulties that I emphasized about simple-minded welfare reform. He focuses on the likelihood that compulsory workfare will worsen the situation of the working poor. He does not allow for the other problem, that many welfare recipients will not be able to land jobs at all. His labor market clears. I think he works on the more interesting part of the story.

It is perhaps not surprising that his work confirms some of the things that I said in the second lecture. He is making explicit the sort of reasoning that lies implicitly behind my remarks. But he also makes clear some things that I had not thought about. For instance, it may matter quite a lot exactly how good a substitute unskilled labor is for skilled labor in the process of production. One could vary that parameter in his model and keep track of the corresponding change in the results. The same goes for variations in the frequency distribution of "child-care costs" in the model. As he says, the cost of child care is not the only deterrent to low-wage work; he makes it stand for all of them, and it would be worth thinking more carefully about some of the others. In both the instances I have mentioned, it is not hard to figure out the rough qualitative character of the answers. The explicit model can help one distinguish the important factors from the unimportant.

A model like this also raises questions that might be answered by a successor model. For example, it would be interesting to extend the Roemer model to one with three or four skill levels, to see how quickly the wage-depressant effect of workfare evaporates as one goes up the skill ladder.

At the end of his comments, Professor Roemer turns to

equality of opportunity and the urgent need to improve the marketable skills of disadvantaged potential workers. He has a very carefully worked-out definition of equal opportunity. He does not elaborate on this in his comment, so I will just take it for granted. The implication is that genuine equality of opportunity would entail compensatory—additional—educational expenditure on the children of low-status families. Slum schools should get more resources than the school on the hill. Merely to say that is to understand how difficult it would be to achieve, and Professor Roemer is no naive optimist. It is interesting that extra expenditure has sometimes been achievable for children with physical disabilities. Apparently socio-economic disabilities do not count. A first step might be to convince voters that they should count, that they are quite real. That might be easier than starting with an abstract question like alternative interpretations of equality of opportunity.

However that might be, I do not see how anyone could quarrel with the substance of Professor Roemer's recommendation that a long-run solution be sought in improving the primary and secondary education available to poor children. Which brings me back almost to where I began this response. A market economy has a hard time dealing humanely with a very wide inequality of earning capacities. Promoting some more humaneness is one possible remedy; reducing the initial inequality of acquired skills is another. That will take a little humaneness, too.

❖ CONTRIBUTORS ❖

Amy Gutmann, Laurance S. Rockefeller University Professor and Director of the University Center for Human Values at Princeton University, is author most recently of *Color Conscious* (with Anthony Appiah, Princeton University Press) and *Democracy and Disagreement* (with Dennis Thompson, Harvard University Press).

Gertrude Himmelfarb is Professor Emeritus at the Graduate School of the City University of New York. Her most recent books are *On Looking into the Abyss: Untimely Thoughts on Culture and Society* (Alfred A. Knopf) and *The De-Moralization of Society: From Victorian Virtues to Modern Values* (Alfred A. Knopf).

Anthony Lewis, a Pulitzer–Prize winning columnist for the *New York Times*, is the author most recently of *Make No Law: The Sullivan Case and the First Amendment* (Random House).

Glenn C. Loury is University Professor, Professor of Economics, and Director of the Institute on Race and Social Division at Boston University. He is the author most recently of *One by One from the Inside Out: Essays and Reviews on Race and Responsibility in America* (The Free Press).

John E. Roemer is Professor of Economics and Director of the Program on Economy, Justice and Society at the University of California, Davis. His most recent books are *Equality of Opportunity* (Harvard University Press) and *Theories of Distributive Justice* (Harvard University Press).

ROBERT M. SOLOW, Institute Professor Emeritus in the Department of Economics at the Massachusetts Institute of Technology is a Nobel–Prize winning macroeconomist with a special interest in the working of the labor market. In the first capacity, he is the author of *Learning from "Learning by Doing"* (Stanford University Press), and in the second, of *The Labor Market As a Social Institution* (Blackwell).